Hiroshima

PERSPECTIVES ON

Hiroshima

Birth of the Nuclear Age

MICHAEL BURGAN

Marshall Cavendish
Benchmark
New York

Marshall Cavendish Benchmark
99 White Plains Road
Tarrytown, NY 10591-5502
www.marshallcavendish.us

Expert Reader: Robert Maddox, Professor Emeritus, Department of History,
Pennsylvania State University, College Park

Library of Congress Cataloging-in-Publication Data

Burgan, Michael.
Hiroshima : birth of the nuclear age / by Michael Burgan.
p. cm. — (Perspectives on)
Includes bibliographical references and index.
Summary: "Provides comprehensive information on the Manhattan Project,
the bombing of Hiroshima, and its legacy"—Provided by the publisher.
ISBN 978-0-7614-4023-9
1. Hiroshima-shi (Japan)—History—Bombardment, 1945.
2. Atomic bomb—United States—History. I. Title.
D767.25.H6B87 2009
940.54'2521954—dc22
2008029249

Editor: Christine Florie
Publisher: Michelle Bisson
Art Director: Anahid Hamparian
Series Designer: Sonia Chaghatzbanian

Photo research by Marybeth Kavanagh

Cover photo by SuperStock, Inc.

The photographs in this book are used by permission and through the courtesy of:
Getty Images: Popperfoto, 2–3; MPI, 28, 59; Thomas D. Mcavoy/Time Life Pictures,
24; March Of Time/Time Life Pictures, 33; National Archives/Time & Life Pictures,
44; Agence France Presse , 48; Los Alamos National Laboratory/Time & Life
Pictures, 49; Paul Popper/Popperfoto, 54; Keystone, 83; *SuperStock*: 8; Age
fotostock, 12; Jack Novak, 62; *Corbis*: 57, 87; epa, 13; Bettmann: 18, 22, 67;
The Image Works: Mary Evans Picture Library, 19; Topham: 36, 40; Photo12, 64;
The Bridgeman Art Library: Private Collection/Roger-Viollet,Paris, 68; *The Granger
Collection, New York*: 72, 73; *AP Photo*: 90; *Photo Researchers, Inc.*: Philippe Psaila, 100.

Printed in Malaysia
1 3 5 6 4 2

Contents

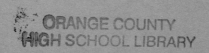

Introduction

W<small>AR PRESENTS A NATION'S LEADERS</small> and citizens with difficult choices and decisions. First they must decide if going to war is even the right thing to do, and if so, what the ultimate goal of the war should be. Once they choose war as the proper course, military officials and government leaders must make decisions about tactics and strategy.

Since the nineteenth century, developments in science and technology have made wars more destructive than ever before. Machine guns, powerful artillery, aircraft, chemical and biological weapons—all have made it possible to kill a large number of people in a short period of time, and often from a great distance. Pilots releasing bombs from thousands of feet in the air may never see the buildings they destroy or the people they kill.

On August 6, 1945, the United States unleashed the most powerful weapon ever used in wartime. A single atomic bomb blew up over the city of Hiroshima, Japan, killing tens of thousands of people immediately. Thousands more died in the weeks, months, and years to come, the victims of radiation.

Scientists from the United States, Great Britain, and other countries worked together to build the atomic bomb.

They knew the atomic bomb could play a role in ending the war. But J. Robert Oppenheimer, who led the scientists who made the bomb, also knew they had also created something extremely dangerous. He cited a line from the Bhagavad-Gita, a Hindu holy text: "Now I am become Death, the destroyer of worlds."

Many of the scientists and leaders who knew about the atomic bomb assumed it would be used against Japan. But some people said the United States could arrange a test bombing to show Japan the tremendous power of the weapon. The results might have been enough to convince the Japanese to end the war. But U.S. civilian leaders decided the atomic bomb had to be dropped on real targets—first Hiroshima, and then the city of Nagasaki. Since the war ended so quickly afterward, most Americans thought this was the right decision. Over time, however, views on dropping the atomic bomb have changed. Historians uncovered facts that most Americans did not know in 1945, or for decades after. The decision to drop the bomb was not just about ending the war. It was meant, in part, to influence postwar relations with the Soviet Union.

World War II continues to engender different perspectives on many issues. But the bombing of Hiroshima may be the one issue most relevant today, when thousands of nuclear weapons are stored around the world and more nations are trying to build them. The nuclear age began with the bombing of Hiroshima, ending one war but raising the threat of deadlier wars to come.

One

A
Special
Mission

EARLY IN THE MORNING OF AUGUST 6, 1945, Colonel Paul Tibbets spoke to his flight crew as they prepared to take off. The men were on board a B-29 bomber plane that Tibbets had named for his mother, Enola Gay. He asked the men, "You know what we're doing today?" The men replied that they were going on a bombing mission. Tibbets said, "Yeah, we're going on a bombing mission, but it's a little bit special." Tibbets knew that he and his men were about to make history. The one bomb on the *Enola Gay* that day was the most powerful weapon ever made—the atomic bomb.

Just over a decade earlier, scientists had learned how to split atoms, tiny particles of the matter composing all earthly substances. Later, scientists learned that splitting the core, or nucleus, of atoms of the element uranium released tremendous amounts of energy. Since 1942 the United States, Great Britain, and Canada had been working together to split atoms of uranium and use the energy created as the destructive force in a new kind of bomb.

This aerial image shows Hiroshima after the *Enola Gay* dropped an atomic bomb on the city on August 6, 1945.

A New Age Begins

The bomb dropped from the *Enola Gay* used a process called fission—the splitting of atomic nuclei (plural of *nucleus*)—to release energy. Later, to create even more powerful bombs, scientists developed bombs that employed fusion, in which the nucleus of a hydrogen atom and the nucleus of an atom from another element were joined together, or fused. Weapons relying on the fusion process were known as hydrogen bombs. Bombs of both types are often called nuclear weapons, because the source of their power is in the nuclei of different atoms. The first use of these weapons in a war, at Hiroshima, Japan, marked the beginning of the nuclear age.

The three countries were part of the Allies—the countries fighting together against Germany in World War II. In Asia the British and Americans were also fighting against Japan, an ally of Germany. The war had started in 1939, when Germany invaded Poland. Now, as Tibbets and his crew prepared for their mission, Germany had recently surrendered. Japan, however, had not given up, even though it had suffered heavy losses. Allied leaders hoped dropping the atomic bomb would save the lives of their troops and end the war.

At 2:45 AM on August 6 the *Enola Gay* took off from Tinian, a small island in the Pacific Ocean. Several other planes flew ahead, checking the weather. Two more B-29s later joined the *Enola Gay* to collect information about the bombing. In less than six hours, the planes would cross the Pacific Ocean and reach Japan.

A City Awakes

On August 6 the morning sun rose over a warm, calm day in Hiroshima, Japan. Across the city people prepared to go to work. Suddenly, around 7 AM, a siren went off. The piercing noise meant enemy planes were on their way, and everyone should find shelter as protection from bombs. All over the country people had gotten used to these sirens. U.S. planes had been bombing the islands of Japan for several months. But when the people of Hiroshima looked up on this morning, all they saw was a weather plane. It flew over the city and then turned away. The city residents came out of their shelters and continued their daily routines.

Around 8 AM the air-raid sirens went off again. Some people went to the shelters, but others thought another weather

A replica of Little Boy, the bomb dropped on Hiroshima, can be found at the National Museum of the United States Air Force, near Dayton, Ohio.

plane was on its way and ignored the alarm. Over their heads, more than 5 miles above the city, the *Enola Gay* approached. At 8:15 the crew released the atomic bomb, which had been nicknamed Little Boy. Attached to a parachute, it slowly drifted down toward Hiroshima. Meanwhile, Colonel Tibbets made a hard turn so the *Enola Gay* could escape the blast from the powerful bomb it had just released.

When Little Boy was about 1,900 feet above the city, it exploded. What people saw and heard that day in Hiroshima depended on where they were. Close to the bomb only an intense flash of light was visible, while farther away, people saw the light and heard an explosion. The color of the flash varied. Some said it was blue, others yellow or red. In Japanese the flash was called *pika* and the explosion *ðon*. Years later, the survivors of the blast still talked about the *pika-ðon* of August 6.

The explosion of the atomic bomb sent out a tremendous wave of heat and energy that vaporized people, animals, and buildings. All that was left of some people were shadows burned into surrounding walls that withstood the blast. Farther away the energy caused terrible burns. A teenage girl named Michiko Yamaoka was so badly burned that a friend did not at first recognize her. She told Michiko, "Miss Yamaoka, you look like a monster." The explosion's intense heat also started fires that raged throughout the city.

Above Hiroshima the *Enola Gay* had managed to fly about 10 miles before the bomb exploded. But even from that distance Tibbets and his crew felt shocks from the blast.

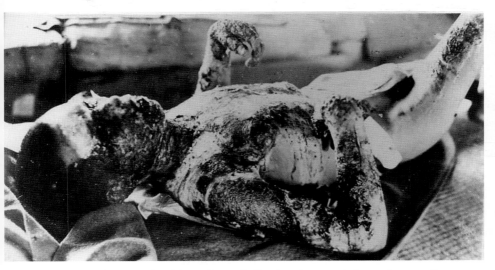

The blast of heat emitted from the exploding bomb severely burned many of its victims.

Two Views of the Bombing

Theodore "Dutch" Van Kirk, crew member of the *Enola Gay*:

All we saw in the airplane was a bright flash. Shortly after that, the first shock wave hit us, and the plane snapped all over . . . the entire city of Hiroshima was covered in black smoke and dust, debris that had been kicked up by the bomb and the blast, and a large white cloud. . . . There was one thought that was uppermost on everyone's mind. Somebody said, and I thought too, "This war is over." You didn't see how anybody . . . could stand up to something like this.

Toyofumi Ogura, Hiroshima resident:

A massive cloud column . . . appeared, boiling violently and seething upward. It was so big it blotted out much of the blue sky. . . . At the moment of the roar and the blast, I had heard tremendous ripping, slamming and crashing sounds as houses and buildings were torn apart. I also thought I heard screams. But these may have simply drifted into my memory later, or been products of my imagination. However, I definitely did hear people crying afterward, "What's that?" "What happened?" And I saw people rushing from their houses out into the streets.

One of the men later told a reporter it felt as if a giant had hit the plane with a telephone pole. But the *Enola Gay* survived the blast and made it safely to its base on Tinian.

Aftermath

On that summer day in Hiroshima as many as 70,000 people died immediately from the detonation of the first atomic bomb. Perhaps 70,000 or more died later, from radiation or the injuries they suffered that day. Despite the destruction of one of their major cities, the Japanese did not surrender. Three days later the Americans dropped a second atomic bomb, on Nagasaki. Within several days after that blast the emperor of Japan said that his country would no longer fight the war. In the United States soldiers and sailors cheered the news. If the atomic bombs had not worked or had not forced Japan to surrender, the Allies would have invaded Japan. The battle could have cost tens of thousands of lives.

Today, the dropping of Little Boy is remembered as the beginning of the nuclear age. After World War II scientists learned how to use the power inside atoms to create electricity and power ships. But that power was also put inside even deadlier bombs than the ones dropped on Japan. Hiroshima remains a warning sign of the dangers of the nuclear age.

Two

A Time of Trouble

DAY AFTER DAY THROUGHOUT THE 1930s, as Americans read their daily papers or listened to the news on the radio, many felt a sense of despair. The decade had begun with the country entering the worst depression, or economic downturn, in U.S. history. Starting in October 1929 the stock market crashed—shares in many companies lost their value, and investors lost money. Soon, banks were failing, unable to pay out the money people had deposited, and millions of people began to lose their jobs.

In November 1932 U.S. voters chose Franklin D. Roosevelt as their president. FDR, as he was called, had campaigned to the theme song "Happy Days Are Here Again," and he had said, "I pledge you, I pledge myself, to a new deal for the American people." The New Deal, he promised, would lead to jobs and security for all.

But even as FDR and Congress worked to create new jobs and aid the poor, the economy continued to struggle. Adding to the hardships at home were increasing problems overseas. The Depression was international, and poor economic conditions led citizens in many countries to embrace

President Franklin Delano Roosevelt (seated far left) visits a Civilian Conservation Corps camp in upstate New York in 1933. The Corps, created by Roosevelt's New Deal, put Americans back to work during the Depression.

leaders with radical ideas—if those leaders promised jobs, national pride, and order.

Troubles Overseas

In January 1933 Adolf Hitler came to power in Germany. He vowed to restore the country's glory, lost as a result of its defeat in World War I and the painful terms of surrender spelled out in the Treaty of Versailles. The treaty had forced Germany to give up land and pay reparations—money for the damage it had caused to other countries during the war. Hitler ignored the treaty's additional terms limiting Germany's future military strength. Soon after coming to power, he told his advisers, "The next five years must be dedicated to the rearmament of the German people." All public programs, he said, had to satisfy that goal.

Within three years Germany had taken back control of the Saar and the Rhineland, two regions it had given up under the Treaty of Versailles. Hitler and his Nazi Party also sent arms to Spain, where a civil war pitted supporters of socialism and democracy against nationalists who wanted strict control of the government. Socialists believe

Adolf Hitler shakes the hands of admiring supporters at Nuremberg in 1933.

Extreme Politics in America

The desire for drastic action during the Depression years led to the growth of political parties and social movements in the United States that shared ideas with the Nazis and Fascists. These included the Silver Shirts, which supported Hitler and shared the Nazis' anti-Semitism—an intense, irrational hatred of Jews. On the other side of the political spectrum, socialism and communism also became more popular. Communists had taken power in Russia in 1917 and created the Soviet Union. Like socialists, they called for government ownership of businesses. But the communists went even further, allowing just one political party, theirs, and seeking limits on personal freedom. In the 1932 presidential election, Socialist and Communist Party candidates combined to win almost one million votes—more than three times the number they had polled in 1928.

that the people, through the government, should own businesses, while democrats favor elected governments that protect individual rights. In Spain both groups opposed the wealthy, who dominated society and tended to support the nationalists.

The nationalists were not unlike Hitler's Nazis (the party name is a short form of the German words for *national* and *socialist*), who believed people should sacrifice their individual freedoms for the good of the country. Hitler backed the Spanish nationalists, as did Italy's Benito Mussolini, who entered the war of Germany's side in 1940. Mussolini's Fascist Party shared similar ideas with the Nazis and Spanish nationalists. All believed a government run by one strong man was better than an elected government that could not keep order.

In Asia the Depression also hit hard in Japan. Prices for rice and silk, two major Japanese exports, fell drastically. At the same time the country struggled to buy the natural resources and finished goods it could only acquire overseas. In rural areas many people faced starvation.

Japan was headed by a monarch, Emperor Hirohito, but the country also had a democratic government that made laws. In the military some officers thought the best way to deal with the Depression and restore Japanese pride was by ending democratic rule. The officers worked to strengthen the power of the emperor, weaken the government, and build a military machine able to secure the natural resources Japan needed to grow. Japanese expansion began in September 1931, as the country took control of large parts of Manchuria, a region in China. To some Japanese military leaders the conquest was necessary to the country's survival.

Emperor Hirohito (above) gave the Japanese military broad powers in running the country.

Nationalist pride gave some officers the sense that they were better than other Asians and had a natural right to others' lands. General Sadao Araki told one international group that Manchuria would "never be allowed to return to Chinese hands," while another Japanese official later wrote that Japan would become the greatest empire on Earth.

Since before World War I the United States had seen Japan as a potential rival in Asia and the Pacific Ocean. The Americans favored what they called the Open Door policy—they wanted all countries to trade freely with China and other nations in the region. The United States controlled the Philippines and several small Pacific islands, and its naval and merchant ships sailed Pacific waters. U.S. leaders feared any Japanese actions that threatened free trade in China or larger U.S. interests in the region. After the Manchuria invasion, Secretary of State Henry Stimson said the Japanese government seemed to be "in the hands of virtually mad dogs." Still, the Americans lacked the military power and the political will to stop the Japanese. Around the world the Manchuria invasion brought protest from some democratic countries but no real action.

A Policy of Isolation

Throughout the 1930s U.S. leaders also worried about events unfolding in Europe. After 1933 President Roosevelt watched with alarm as Hitler began to rearm Germany, take back the land the country had lost, and sign a treaty of cooperation with Japan. Roosevelt genuinely hated war, as he had seen the destruction in Europe caused by World War I. And he did not want to lose the support of U.S. lawmakers and voters who favored neutrality. In 1935 and 1936 the president signed into law bills that declared U.S. neutrality in foreign conflicts. But Roosevelt also saw the danger of the rising power of nationalists and fascists, especially in Germany and Japan. In January 1936 he said there was "growing ill-will . . . increasing armaments . . . shortening tempers—a situation which has in it many of the elements that lead to the tragedy of general war."

The backers of U.S. neutrality were called isolationists. They hoped to keep the United States separated from the

A soldier grabs a sign from a demonstrating isolationist in front of the White House in Washington, D.C.

growing problems of the world around them. Their leaders included Senators Hiram Johnson of California and Gerald Nye of North Dakota. Some isolationists thought the United States had made a mistake by entering World War I in 1917, and they did not want to take part in new foreign wars. Nye in particular was upset by the vast amounts of money U.S. companies had made selling arms during the war. Nye believed that "war and preparation for war is not

America First

The isolationist movement reached a peak in 1940 with the creation of the America First Committee. The group was dedicated to keeping the United States out of the war in Europe. Its most famous member was Charles A. Lindbergh. The aviator made history in 1927 when he became the first person to fly solo across the Atlantic Ocean. During the 1930s Lindbergh spent several years in Europe. He was impressed by Nazi Germany's growing military might and its strong opposition to the Soviet Union. Lindbergh disliked the Soviets and their communist government, and he had isolationist views even before the America First Committee formed. In 1940 he said the United States should not get involved in "the internal affairs of Europe; they never were, and never will be, carried on according to our desires."

a matter of national honor and national defense, but a matter of profit for the few," and the idea angered him. Other isolationists thought softening the devastating effects of the Great Depression at home was more important than sorting out problems abroad. And some isolationists were pacifists, people who believe all wars are wrong.

The isolationist feelings remained strong as the threat of war continued to grow. In August 1937 Japan invaded China again, seeking to extend its control beyond Manchuria. Less than a year later Germany took control of Austria without firing a shot and made plans to seize part of Czechoslovakia, where many German-speaking people lived. By March 1939 all of Czechoslovakia was in German hands, and that September German tanks and soldiers swarmed into Poland, marking the start of World War II in Europe.

Throughout this period of growing turmoil President Roosevelt spoke out more strongly about the dangers he saw. In October 1937, responding to Japan's newest aggression in China, he told the nation that no country could truly isolate itself from world events. He believed "the peace, the freedom, the security of ninety percent . . . of the world is being jeopardized by the remaining ten percent who are threatening a breakdown of all international order and law." Still, even after the German invasion of Poland, isolationist lawmakers refused to back down.

Entering the War

After September 1939 President Roosevelt clearly wanted to aid Great Britain, France, and the other nations fighting in Europe. Like the United States, Britain and France had democratic governments. They stood for personal freedom and the rule of law against the Nazi values of totalitarian rule and dominance of others. Roosevelt convinced Congress to let the French and British purchase some U.S. weapons. He then won approval in March 1941 for Lend-Lease, a program that allowed Great Britain and the other Allied nations to purchase even more weapons on credit. After June 1941 the Soviet Union became one of the Allies, as it faced a surprise German attack that drew it into the battle against Hitler.

By this time tensions were rising between the United States and Japan. German victories in France and the Netherlands in 1940 meant that those countries had lost effective control over their colonies in Asia. Japan stepped in, sending troops into the French colony of Vietnam and making plans to control Dutch and British colonies in the region. The Japanese also signed a treaty with Germany and Italy. Each pledged to help the others if any of the three went to war with another nation. Japan hoped this arrangement would discourage the United States from taking military steps against its expansion.

Throughout 1940 the United States tried to weaken Japan by limiting trade with the resource-poor nation. Roosevelt hoped that without access to U.S. scrap iron and fuel for its airplanes, the Japanese would consider reversing its push into other lands. Instead, the Japanese became more determined to seize Asian colonies that had valuable natural resources.

By 1941 U.S. intelligence officials had cracked a code Japan used to send messages between Tokyo and Washington, D.C., where important Japanese officials were stationed. The two countries were still trying to peacefully settle their differences, but time was running out. Then, in November 1941, the Americans decoded a message indicating that the Japanese were preparing for war. Henry Stimson, then FDR's secretary of war, later wrote, "Japan had already set in motion the wheels of her war machine, and she had decided not to stop short of war with the United States if by November 25 we had not agreed to her demands." Those demands included restoring trade and giving Japan the right to attack China from Vietnam, if necessary. The United States made its own offers, knowing that Japan might soon attack U.S. bases in the Philippines or British and Dutch colonial ports.

On December 7, 1941, when Japan indeed took action, it ignored those targets. Instead, on a quiet Sunday morning

Warships blaze in Pearl Harbor after the surprise attack by the Japanese on December 7, 1941.

hundreds of Japanese warplanes bombarded the U.S. naval base at Pearl Harbor, Hawaii. The surprise raid shocked most U.S. citizens, as it killed more than 2,400 Americans and sank or damaged almost twenty naval ships. Shortly thereafter the Japanese attacked the Philippines and several small U.S. possessions in the Pacific. Japanese leaders had decided that the United States would never let it achieve its aim of domination over East Asia. So Japan had attacked first, hoping to cripple the U.S. naval forces in the Pacific. With the strike on Pearl Harbor, the United States was drawn into World War II. President Roosevelt told the country, "I have directed that all measures be taken for our defense. . . . No matter how long it may take us . . . the American people, in their righteous might, will win through absolute victory."

Three

The Manhattan Project

EVEN BEFORE PEARL HARBOR WAS ATTACKED, as the threat of another world war grew, President Roosevelt had taken a bold step to confront the danger posed by Nazi Germany. The U.S. government, along with the British, was funding research on a new weapon, the atomic bomb. The idea that atoms could be split, unleashing massive amounts of energy, had first been discussed several decades before. Now Roosevelt and others hoped to use that destructive power against Germany—assuming the Germans didn't unlock the secrets for building an atomic bomb before they did.

Theories and Research

The scientist Albert Einstein helped create modern physics with his ideas on the nature of time and space. Einstein also saw that matter—solids, liquids, gases—and energy are related—they are actually the same thing, just in different forms. And he realized, as he later said, "that very small amounts of mass [of matter] may be converted into a very large amount of energy and vice versa." He expressed this idea in his famous formula, $E = mc^2$: energy equals mass times the speed of light (a constant) multiplied by itself.

Einstein introduced the first of his ideas on energy and matter in 1905. In the years that followed, other scientists explored the nature of atoms. Within an atom is a center called the nucleus. The composition of the nucleus varies from one element to another. Hydrogen, for example, has a nucleus of a single particle called a proton. Protons have a positive electrical charge. Circling around the hydrogen nucleus is an electron, a particle with a negative charge. Some elements have much heavier atoms, with more protons in the nucleus, along with particles called neutrons, which have the same mass as a proton but no electrical charge. The natural element with the heaviest atom is uranium. The nucleus of a uranium atom has 92 protons and a varying number of neutrons, usually 146.

Throughout the 1930s scientists around the world studied the effect of bombarding the nuclei of uranium atoms with neutrons. In Germany in 1938 Otto Hahn and Fritz Strassmann sent a stream of neutrons into uranium and produced the lighter element barium. The process also released energy. Hahn and Strassmann had stumbled onto nuclear fission, a way to unlock the energy stored in atoms.

First Steps Toward a Bomb

Early in 1939 Hahn and Strassmann published articles explaining their work. Other scientists saw that fission might lead to new sources of energy for peaceful purposes, such as generating electricity or powering ships. Some also saw that fission could lead to the development of powerful new weapons. But few, if any, thought that such a weapon could be developed quickly, and some believed they would never be built.

By this time Albert Einstein was living and working in the United States. He was one of many Jewish scientists who had fled Germany and the lands it controlled, fearing the anti-Semitic policies of the Nazis. Another was Hungarian-born Leo Szilard, who taught at New York's Columbia University and, like Einstein and many others, had become a U.S. citizen. Szilard was one of the scientists who doubted that fission could lead to a new weapon. Still, he wasn't sure—and even before the start of World War II in September 1939, he feared what would happen if Nazi Germany developed such a weapon before other countries did. Hitler's seemingly unending push to control more of Europe would be almost unstoppable.

In July 1939 Szilard met with Einstein, seeking his help. Szilard worried about Germany taking control of uranium ore in Africa, and he feared German research on an atomic bomb. Szilard asked Einstein to write a letter to President Roosevelt. The world-famous German-born physicist was widely respected; his opinion might influence FDR to see the importance of funding research into the possible creation of an atomic bomb. Einstein was a pacifist, but he, like Szilard, saw the danger of a German military equipped with atomic weapons. Einstein agreed to write the letter.

In his letter Einstein said that recent research indicated that an atomic bomb was a possibility. Just one of those bombs, Einstein warned, could be "carried by boat and exploded in a port [which] might very well destroy the whole port together with some of the surrounding territory." Einstein said Germany could be preparing to work on such a bomb, and it was already restricting the sale of uranium

Albert Einstein (left) and Leo Szilard reenact the signing of their letter to President Roosevelt that warned of Germany's interest in building an atomic weapon.

from lands it controlled in Czechoslovakia. The scientist asked Roosevelt to make sure the United States had a reliable supply of uranium and to fund research for developing an atomic bomb.

The Uranium Committee

Einstein wrote his letter in August, and it reached Roosevelt in October. The president was not a scientist, but he

Later Regrets

Leo Szilard and Albert Einstein based their desire for atomic research on one major fact: they feared what Germany would do with a bomb. But even before the first atomic bomb was dropped on Hiroshima, Szilard had doubts about the morality of using it. He thought the scientists who created the bomb should have a greater say in its possible use—an idea both U.S. civilian and military leaders rejected. After the war Szilard strongly opposed efforts to devise "superbombs" that would use nuclear fusion to create even more destructive weapons. Einstein did not work on the atomic bomb project, but he later said about his 1939 letter to FDR, "If I had known that the Germans would not succeed in constructing the atom bomb, I would never have lifted a finger." He, like Szilard, opposed the dropping of the atomic bombs on Japan and the development of the superbomb.

understood what Einstein was suggesting. The possibility of making an atomic weapon was too real to ignore, and letting Germany build the first one was too risky. But Roosevelt was not ready to order a massive research program for building such a weapon.

The president's first step was to set up a temporary committee designed to study what role, if any, the recent research on the fission of uranium might have in national defense. This Uranium Committee, as it was called, first met in October 1939. Szilard was on it, along with Edward Teller, a physicist already doing work on uranium fission at New York's Columbia University with Enrico Fermi, who in 1938 had received the Nobel Prize in Physics.

Fermi's research dealt with chain reactions—a process that would play a key role in creating an atomic bomb. When one atom is split after being bombarded by neutrons, it releases more neutrons, along with energy. Those neutrons can then split other atoms of the original material, and the process keeps repeating, setting up a chain reaction. Fermi and his team knew this was the theory behind splitting enough uranium atoms to make a bomb, but they had not proved it would work as a practical matter.

Early in 1940 the Uranium Committee managed to send $6,000 to Columbia University to fund Fermi's work. The committee was then made a part of the National Defense Research Committee (NDRC). This new, permanent group was set up to look at various scientific projects that could be useful during wartime. Still, work on testing the theory went slowly. Fermi, at least at first, wasn't primarily concerned with using fission as the source of energy in

Enrico Fermi, an Italian-American nuclear physicist, conducted research on chain reactions that played a major role in the creation of the atomic bomb.

a weapon. His interest was in creating nuclear power or radioactive treatments for medicine.

In Great Britain, however, work had progressed a little further, and in 1941 a committee there released the so-called MAUD report. The report summarized the ideas of several

Danger from Foreigners?

Wartime can lead to suspicion of foreigners, especially if they come from countries that are or could be enemies. American and British policies kept foreign-born scientists and engineers from working on the development of radar and other high-priority defense projects. As the first work on atomic research began, some U.S. military and civilian officials worried about the role played by foreign scientists on that project, even ones who, like Einstein, Szilard, and the Italian-born Fermi, had become U.S. citizens. The officials were partly concerned about how Congress and the American people might react if the project failed or if technical secrets reached Germany. The foreign scientists might be blamed, and the officials would then be blamed for using them. But the foreign scientists were also among the most knowledgeable in atomic research, and they played an enormous role in developing the atomic bomb.

scientists, indicating that 25 pounds of uranium could be used to create a bomb "equivalent as regards destructive effect to 1,800 tons of T.N.T. and would also release large quantities of radioactive substance, which would make places near to where the bomb exploded dangerous to human life for a long period." Preparing the uranium so it could be used for a bomb would probably take a little more than two years.

In July 1941 Vannevar Bush, the head of the NDRC, received a copy of the MAUD Report. Bush met with President Roosevelt in October to discuss the research and what it meant for the United States. Clearly, if the British had progressed to the point of describing a workable bomb, the Germans could be doing so as well. FDR decided to ask the British to work with the United States on an atomic bomb and to make the project a top priority. "Time," he told Bush, "is very much of the essence."

The Manhattan Project

Roosevelt chose Bush, along with Secretary of War Stimson and several other officials, to lead the atomic bomb project. Bush, physicist James Conant, and General Leslie R. Groves took control of the day-to-day affairs. The project was given the code name S-1. At first the president wanted Bush and his team to merely conduct more research, though with much greater funding than before. Roosevelt stressed the need for both secrecy—so the Germans would not find out about the work—and speed. The research would be conducted at universities across the United States and at new labs built by the Army's Corps of Engineers.

The Japanese attack on Pearl Harbor on December 7, 1941, gave a new urgency to the effort, and just a few days later the United States was at war with Germany as well. Going into 1942 some U.S. atomic scientists feared that the Germans were already ahead in the race to build the new bomb.

In the summer of 1942 the work on the atomic bomb received a new name. In August the army set up some of its operations for the project in New York City and formed the Manhattan Engineering District. That name was supposed to hide the fact that the real work going on involved uranium fission. Soon, the work to build an atomic bomb was called the Manhattan Project. General Groves was put in charge of the Manhattan Project, though he worked closely with James Conant.

Breakthrough in Chicago

Although the enterprise was called the Manhattan Project, some of the most important research for building an atomic bomb was going on at the University of Chicago. In an old squash court under the stands of the school's football stadium, Enrico Fermi, Leo Szilard, and others were trying to create the first sustainable atomic chain reaction. Their work involved building a pile, or stack, of tons of uranium; with so much of the element, the scientists would not have to bombard it with neutrons, as some neutrons would escape from the atoms naturally. The uranium was inserted into almost 400 tons of graphite bricks. The graphite increased the fission of the uranium atoms, while rods of the element cadmium absorbed the neutrons released by the uranium. The removeable cadmium rods let the scientists control how many neutrons were produced.

Wartime secrecy did not allow for photographs of the completed reactor. This sketch depicts the layers of graphite and uranium used to build it.

On December 2, 1942, the scientists believed there was enough uranium and graphite in place to begin a sustained chain reaction. The cadmium control rods were slowly removed so the neutrons could move freely through the pile. The number of neutrons grew as more and more uranium atoms were split. The rods came out completely, and Fermi announced success—the chain reaction was self-sustaining or, as the scientists said, "critical." Sliding the cadmium rods back into the pile ended the experiment.

Sending word of the successful experiment back to Washington, Manhattan Project scientist Arthur Compton used the code phrase, "The Italian navigator has just landed in the New World." The scientists in Chicago applauded their success, but Leo Szilard was not happy. The man who had done so much to prod the United States into conducting atomic research now had doubts about the morality of the work. He knew the amount of destruction that just a single bomb could cause. Szilard looked at Fermi and said that December 2, 1942, would be remembered as a "black day in the history of mankind."

Four

War on Several Fronts

AFTER THE PEARL HARBOR ATTACK, while the top-secret Manhattan Project picked up speed, the U.S. government and the
American people carried out the war against Japan. Although
the planners of the Manhattan Project were most concerned
about Germany's potential development of an atomic bomb,
Japan was a more immediate military concern.

Suspicions at Home

The surprise Japanese attack stirred fears in the United
States that Japanese Americans might side with Japan and
try to hurt the U.S. war effort. Even before the attack the U.S.
government had studied this possibility, especially along the
West Coast, where most of the country's Japanese Americans
lived. A report issued in November 1941 for President
Roosevelt said that the children of Japanese immigrants,
called nisei, were almost all loyal Americans "eager to show
this loyalty." The report said the Japanese Americans would
not start an armed uprising; only a few Japanese, mostly
sent as secret agents by the current Japanese government,
posed a danger to the country.

But in the weeks after the Pearl Harbor attack, the fear of Japanese disloyalty grew along the West Coast. The war had increased the racial tensions and prejudice that had existed for decades in that part of the country. To some Americans the Japanese, like other Asian immigrants, seemed too foreign to blend into the United States. Whereas the majority of Americans were Christian, the Japanese primarily practiced Buddhism. The Japanese were said to lack personal morals and to be likely to commit crimes. The Japanese also came from a country without a strong tradition of democratic government so, some Americans argued, they could not truly understand the American political system. The Japanese stirred economic jealousy as well. Many had bought land and created successful farms. Others opened profitable businesses. Anti-Japanese forces suggested the Japanese were taking jobs or income from "real" Americans.

Throughout the early 1900s anti-Japanese attitudes had led to the passage of national laws that limited the number of Japanese immigrants allowed to enter the country and their ability to become U.S. citizens. Laws passed in California and other western states also restricted their ability to buy land. The distrust of Japanese Americans exploded after the Pearl Harbor attack, and many Americans did not care if they were citizens or not. The *Los Angeles Times* wrote, "A viper is nonetheless a viper wherever the egg is hatched—so a Japanese American, born of Japanese parents—grows up to be a Japanese, not an American."

The combination of racism and genuine concern for national security during wartime led President Roosevelt to take a drastic step. Going against the suggestions of some of his advisers, who believed the Japanese Americans were not a threat, the president signed Executive Order 9066. The order gave the military the power to remove Japanese Americans from their homes and place them in "relocation centers," which were also called internment camps. The order applied to U.S. citizens of Japanese descent as well as to legal aliens. The government did not attempt to separate actual potential enemy agents from loyal citizens and residents. And Roosevelt did not give the Japanese any legal

Japanese-American women meet outside their living quarters at the Heart Mountain Relocation Camp in Wyoming.

way to challenge their forced removal from their homes and relocation to distant, isolated camps, surrounded by armed guards. Still, most Japanese did not want to cause trouble or stir up even deeper hatred, and they peacefully obeyed the order. Some lived in the camps for several years, denied their freedoms and rights as Americans.

On to Los Alamos

By the time of the first sustained chain reaction in Chicago, the Japanese internment camps were in full operation. The camps seemed to end the threat of widespread Japanese espionage, and in the Pacific, U.S. forces were holding their own, after a major victory near the Midway Islands. For President Roosevelt Germany was still the number-one concern. By the end of 1942 the Soviet Union was fighting the Germans along what was called the Eastern Front, a line roughly from Leningrad (St. Petersburg) south to the Black Sea. U.S. and British forces were also fighting the Germans in North Africa.

The Germans were, as the Allies expected, working on their own atomic bomb. The desire to beat the Germans in this potentially deadly race kept the Manhattan Project scientists motivated. What they did not learn until late in the war was that they were advancing much more quickly than were the Germans.

Starting in February 1943 the location of the major Allied research switched to a remote spot in the mountains outside Albuquerque, New Mexico. General Groves named the American physicist J. Robert Oppenheimer as the head of a new laboratory built there, the Los Alamos Scientific Laboratory. Oppenheimer's task was to design and build a

Different Views on Relocation

On March 6, 1942, the *San Francisco News* offered its opinion on the relocation of local Japanese Americans:

Although their removal ... may inconvenience them somewhat, even work serious hardships upon some, they must certainly recognize the necessity of clearing the coastal combat areas of all possible ... saboteurs. ... That is a clear-cut policy easily understood. Its execution should be supported by all citizens of whatever racial background, but especially it presents an opportunity to the people of an enemy race to prove their spirit of co-operation and keep their relations with the rest of the population of this country on the firm ground of friendship. Every indication has been given that the transfer will be made with the least possible hardship.

Yoshiko Uchida was a teenager when she and her family were forced to leave their homes. Their first stop was Tanforan Racetrack, which had been turned into a temporary camp for Japanese Americans before they went to the relocation centers. She later wrote about her experiences:

The stall was about ten by twenty feet and empty except for three folded Army cots lying on the floor. Dust, dirt, and wood shavings covered the linoleum that had been laid over the manure-covered boards, the smell of horses hung in the air, and the whitened corpses of many insects still clung to the hastily white-washed walls. . . . We spent most of the evening talking about food and the lack of it, a concern that grew obsessive over the next few weeks when we were constantly hungry.

The physicist J. Robert Oppenheimer was named the head of the Los Alamos Scientific Laboratory.

workable atomic bomb as quickly as possible, drawing on the work of Fermi, Szilard, and many others.

Oppenheimer recruited scientists from around the country. Some did not like the idea of working under military control. They wanted the freedom scientists had in private labs, to follow their research where it took them, so Los Alamos remained under civilian control throughout the war. But General Groves stuck to his guns on "compartmentalization" — keeping the scientists working on one part of the Manhattan Project from knowing what others were doing. The general said this policy made the scientists work more efficiently, though his real concern was security.

Compartmentalization, however, frustrated scientists used to sharing ideas and coming up with new theories triggered by the work of others. Leo Szilard later admitted that in their effort to build the bomb as quickly as possible, he and other scientists ignored Groves's rule. Compartmentalization reflected the tensions between some of the scientists and the military, and their views would continue to differ.

At Los Alamos Oppenheimer and his various teams of scientists worked on two different bomb designs. One used plutonium, a radioactive element created when uranium is bombarded with neutrons. The bomb used high explosives to crush a piece of plutonium, causing what is called an

Two scientists at Los Alamos Scientific Laboratory haul out radioactive material as part of their research.

Lingering Effects of Nuclear Work

While work began at Los Alamos, new facilities were also built in Hanford, Washington, and Oak Ridge, Tennessee. Hanford became the source of most of the plutonium used during the Manhattan Project, while Oak Ridge provided a special form of uranium, U-235, that created a rapid chain reaction. One of today's concerns about nuclear weapons and nuclear power is that the process of making the weapons or generating power leaves highly radio-active waste materials that pose health hazards for thousands of years. Hanford, where nuclear production went on for decades, still has millions of gallons of radioactive wastewater on the site. The U.S. government is trying to turn the waste into glass, which can be more safely stored than the water. At Oak Ridge scientists are exploring new ways to safely recycle nuclear waste. But in the meantime people living near waste sites fear radiation could contaminate drinking water and soil.

implosion. The implosion then released the energy inside the plutonium. The other bomb used uranium and a "gun" that fired one piece of the material at another. The collision of the two pieces of uranium at high speeds started a chain reaction and created explosive power.

The World Outside Los Alamos

As the work went on in New Mexico and at other Manhattan Project sites, the Allies were making gains on the battlefield. In July 1943 U.S. and British troops invaded Italy, securing Mussolini's surrender in September. Also in 1943 the Soviet Union won the advantage on the Eastern Front and began pushing back the Germans. In June 1944 British, American, and Canadian forces landed in France and started to force a German retreat. In the Pacific the U.S. military was slowly pushing westward, following its strategy of taking island bases from the Japanese so it could eventually launch air raids on Japan itself.

By the fall of 1944 Roosevelt and the British prime minister, Winston Churchill, were increasingly sure the Allies would defeat Germany. In September they secretly met at Roosevelt's family estate in Hyde Park, New York, to discuss the atomic bomb. The two leaders agreed that they would not seek any international agreements regarding the use and control of atomic weapons. They also decided that "when a 'bomb' is finally available, it might perhaps, after mature consideration, be used against the Japanese." The defeat of Germany would not end the work on the Manhattan Project.

In the months that followed, Roosevelt won reelection for the third time. Thus, as he began his fourth term, he was already the longest-serving president in U.S. history. Entering 1945, his health worsened, and on April 12, 1945, he died at his vacation home in Warm Springs, Georgia. Vice President Harry Truman was quickly sworn in as president. Truman knew that the war in Europe was almost over. Soviet troops were closing in on Germany's capital, Berlin, from the east, while U.S. and other Allied troops were moving through Germany from other directions. But the new president didn't know about the Manhattan Project and the atomic bomb. On Truman's first day as president, Secretary of War Stimson merely told Truman he wanted to discuss "a most urgent matter."

Almost two weeks later Stimson and Groves met with Truman. Stimson handed the president a report to read. It said, in part, "Within four months, we shall in all probability have completed the most terrible weapon ever known in human history, one bomb of which could destroy a whole city." Although the British had helped build this new weapon, only the United States could produce a bomb—for the time being. Stimson predicted that the Soviet Union would have the skills in a few years. Groves then went over the details of the Manhattan Project with the president. He told the president that a uranium gun-style bomb would be ready around August 1 and would not need to be tested. The plutonium implosion bomb would be ready sooner but would need to be tested before being put to use in combat. Stimson suggested that a new committee be formed to help Truman decide whether the bomb should be used and what its use might mean. Truman agreed. Using such a destructive weapon, he knew, would be a major decision, and he would need plenty of advice. But the decision of when to use the bomb—if it were to be used at all—would ultimately be Truman's.

Considering the Soviet Union

Since the end of 1944 Stimson had been increasingly concerned about the Soviet Union. Although it was an ally against Germany, its postwar desires contradicted U.S. goals. Afraid of future attacks from Germany or other countries to its west, Soviet leader Joseph Stalin wanted a buffer of nations it could control, preferably with communist governments. Spreading communism around the world was a stated Soviet goal. So was weakening capitalist, democratic countries, which were seen as natural foes of communism. The United States, on the other hand, wanted to limit the spread of communism and promote democracy as it inevitably stepped in to help rebuild Germany and other countries ravaged by the war.

Vannevar Bush and James Conant had been discussing for months whether the British and Americans should tell Stalin about the Manhattan Project. They also thought some sort of international committee should oversee the use of nuclear weapons after the war. The two men did not know about Roosevelt and Churchill's secret Hyde Park agreement. Bush in particular worried that keeping the bomb a secret might seem threatening to the Soviets. Stalin might fear the bomb would be used against his country after the war. Better to be open, Bush believed, than to create new tensions and a race between the Americans and the Soviets to build more and bigger atomic weapons they might use against each other.

British prime minister Winston Churchill, U.S. president Franklin Delano Roosevelt, and Russian leader Joseph Stalin meet to discuss postwar Europe at the Yalta Conference.

In February 1945 Roosevelt, Stalin, and Churchill had met in the Soviet city of Yalta to discuss their plans for postwar Europe. While meeting with Churchill in private, Roosevelt brought up the idea of telling Stalin about the bomb. Churchill said no, and FDR dropped the issue. After FDR's death, Truman showed no desire to tell the Soviets. The bomb would remain a secret—for the time being.

Five

The Nuclear Age Begins

WITHIN WEEKS OF TAKING OFFICE, President Truman was able to join the Allies and millions of people around the world in celebrating some good news. On May 8, 1945, Germany surrendered. Now, the Allies' full attention could turn to Japan, which was already facing destructive bombing raids from U.S. planes. The planes often dropped incendiary bombs, a tactic called firebombing. As the name implies, the bombs created huge fires when they hit their targets. The resulting blazes were called firestorms.

The Interim Committee

Just after Germany's defeat, Stimson's new committee went to work to discuss the use of the atomic bomb against Japan. The Interim Committee, as it was called, included Stimson, Vannevar Bush, James Conant, and James Byrnes, who was slated to become the next secretary of state. An advisory committee of four scientists, including J. Robert Oppenheimer and Enrico Fermi, also took part. At the first meeting Stimson said, "Gentlemen, it is our responsibility to recommend action that may turn the course of civilization."

Firebombing

The Allies first used incendiary bombs against Germany in July 1943, in a devastating attack on Hamburg. About 30,000 civilians died in the raid. In February 1945 an equally deadly firestorm destroyed most of Dresden. The firebombing there and in Japan (right) stirred some controversy then and now. Although most of the cities attacked had some military targets, great numbers of civilians were killed. A March 1945 raid on Tokyo left 83,000 people dead. Some U.S. leaders saw the attacks as a key way to weaken the enemy's will to fight. But Secretary of War Henry Stimson was bothered by the number of civilian deaths caused by the firebombing. He feared the Allies were committing acts almost as bad as Hitler's slaughter of innocents across Europe. (This included the killing of 6 million Jews, a mass murder now known as the Holocaust.) But as historian Thomas Searle said in 2005, "At this stage everybody had been burning down cities. The Americans certainly weren't out of step in that

sense." Still, the firebombing, like dropping the atomic bomb after it, made some people ask whether there should be limits on what a country does to win a war.

Stimson and others U.S. leaders who had been involved with the Manhattan Project from the start had one basic assumption: if the bomb were ready before the end of the war, it would be used in some form. The real questions were, What was the best way to show the power of the bomb so Japan would surrender? And if a direct bombing of Japan were launched, what were the best possible targets? The committee also considered the role the bomb would play in U.S.–Soviet relations through the end of the war and afterward. Once again it was recommended that Stalin not be told about the bomb. Byrnes, in later comments, suggested that if the United States had exclusive control of atomic weapons, it would have a better chance of getting what it wanted from the Soviets in Europe.

The project scientists, as Oppenheimer later told the committee, disagreed over how to use the bomb. The opinions "range from the proposal of a purely technical demonstration to that of the military application best designed to induce surrender." The demonstration would be some public test in a remote area, to show the Japanese the bomb's destructive power. Oppenheimer noted that the scientists who wanted a technical demonstration also wanted to outlaw any future use of atomic weapons. He and the other three scientists working with the Interim Committee, however, favored "direct military use" of the bomb against Japan.

By the time Oppenheimer issued his report, the Interim Committee had decided that the bomb should be used without warning against a factory involved in producing arms. The committee realized that workers living near the plant would be killed as well, including those who would be affected after the actual blast by radiation. The committee also hoped the tremendous blast of light and the destruction from a single bomb would have a psychological effect, weakening the Japanese will to fight.

Roosevelt adviser James Byrnes, secretary of state, left the committee meeting of June 1 to give the results to President Truman. The president, Byrnes later said, "with reluctance . . . had to agree, that he could think of no alternative" to using the atomic bomb on Japan. The committee merely affirmed what Truman had already decided. To Truman the bomb offered a way to end the war quickly and hopefully end the need for the Allies to launch a ground

After succeeding President Roosevelt during the last months of World War II, President Harry Truman made the decision to drop the atomic bomb on Hiroshima.

invasion of Japan. In the weeks to come he would hear estimates of about 31,000 U.S. casualties in just the first month of an invasion; another estimate was almost four times higher.

None of the advisers, however, knew for sure how bloody such a battle would be. And not all agreed an invasion was necessary. General Curtis LeMay, who was in charge of the firebombing raids, thought the continued heavy use of air power would force Japan to surrender. A naval blockade, already in place, would also help, as it prevented Japan from getting vital supplies from overseas. But the most common opinion was that a land invasion was a necessity.

Different Opinions

Going into June 1945, Leo Szilard and some other scientists still hoped to stop the military use of atomic weapons. They feared the United States would lose the moral authority to later set up international controls on nuclear weapons. Even the scientists who supported using the bomb against Japan feared there would be limited control of such weapons in the future, and the idea worried them. One committee of scientists, led by physicist James Franck, issued a report airing these concerns. The Soviet Union and other nations would be shocked by a surprise attack, and "it may be very difficult to persuade the world that a nation which was capable of secretly preparing and suddenly releasing a[n atomic] weapon . . . is to be trusted in its proclaimed desire of having such weapons abolished by international agreement." To bolster the chances of postwar control, some scientists again said the Soviet Union should be informed about the bomb. Late in June the Interim Committee said the United States should consider telling the Soviets about the Manhattan Project, without giving details, if the right opportunity should present itself. The committee, however, neglected to define "right opportunity."

One government official on the Interim Committee also expressed doubts about the decision to drop an atomic bomb without warning. Ralph Bard was the undersecretary of the navy. In late June he suggested giving Japan a few days' warning before using the bomb. He wrote, "The position of the United States as a great humanitarian nation and the fair play attitude of our people generally is responsible in the main for this feeling." Bard also thought that some members of the Japanese government might be ready to end the war. His views, though, did not carry any weight with Truman and Stimson, who were determined to use the bomb, as already decided.

Trinity and Potsdam

By mid-July 1945 action was taking place on two fronts some 5,000 miles apart. Near Alamogordo, New Mexico, at a spot Oppenheimer named Trinity, the U.S. government was preparing to test a plutonium implosion atomic bomb. Meanwhile, in Potsdam, Germany, Truman, Churchill, and Stalin were about to meet to discuss the war with Japan and postwar issues. Truman had delayed this meeting, hoping the Trinity test would be completed beforehand. Instead, on July 16, he received the first coded message about the test. More details of its success would filter into Potsdam in the days to come.

At Alamogordo, at 5:30 AM on July 16, the first explosion of an atomic weapon created a flash of light seen 100 miles away and a blast of sound heard even farther away than that. General Thomas Farrell witnessed the test and

In July 1945 the Trinity atomic test took place near Alamogordo, New Mexico.

later said, "It was a great new force to be used for good or for evil. There was a feeling in that shelter that those concerned with its nativity [birth] should dedicate their lives to the mission that it would always be used for good and never for evil."

In Potsdam Truman later learned that the test blast had a force equal to between 15,000 and 20,000 tons of TNT. In a letter General Groves described how the explosion ripped apart a steel cylinder weighing 220 tons, which had been set up one-half mile from the blast center. No one at Trinity expected that kind of damage. The Manhattan Project members had not even known whether their device would work. Now they knew it was even more powerful than they had imagined.

A few days later Truman made the final decision to use the atomic bomb against Japan in the coming weeks. Truman also hinted to Stalin that the United States had a new weapon that could help end the war. The president, however, did not mention atomic power, and he had no plans to share any more information with the Soviets. He and Secretary of State Byrnes were growing increasingly suspicious of Stalin and had their doubts about whether the Soviet leader would keep all the promises he had made. Yet at Potsdam, Truman welcomed Soviet help against Japan. Stalin agreed he would send Soviet troops into Manchuria by August 15 if the war had not ended. That, Truman believed, would be the end of the Japanese, if they had not already surrendered by then.

As the Potsdam conference came to an end, Great Britain, the United States, and their Asian ally China issued a statement. This document, known as the Potsdam Declaration,

At the Potsdam Conference in 1945 Joseph Stalin (right) agreed to aid the United States in its fight against Japan.

said, in part, "We call upon the government of Japan to proclaim now the unconditional surrender of all Japanese armed forces, and to provide proper and adequate assurances of their good faith in such action. The alternative for Japan is prompt and utter destruction."

Atomic Weapons in Japan

While the Allies were worried about Germany building an atomic bomb, Japan was conducting its own fission research as well. The program began in 1940, with the major push coming in 1943, even though some Japanese scientists said it would take ten years to build a bomb. Work was still proceeding in April 1945, when U.S. air raids destroyed the main research facilities. Information about the program was not widely known for several decades, as the Japanese, victims of the first atomic bomb, seemed unwilling to talk about their interest in developing the weapon. Since 1956 the country has officially promised never to build nuclear weapons or allow them to be stored in Japan.

By the end of the Potsdam Conference Japan's leaders disagreed on what to do next. Some, such as Foreign Minister Shigenori Togo, thought Japan had already lost the war. He wrote to a Japanese diplomat, "We are now secretly giving consideration to terminating the war because of the pressing situation which confronts Japan both at home and abroad." Another message from Togo suggested the emperor himself wanted to end the war quickly (though some historians today doubt that). On the other side of the issue were some military leaders who wanted to fight on at all costs. And on July 17, even Togo said the government would not consider unconditional surrender. Allied leaders, thanks to the breaking of Japanese codes, knew about this debate raging in Japan. They could see that while some Japanese were tiring of the war, the Allies could not count on its swift end. And soon the Japanese rejected the Potsdam Declaration.

Dropping Little Boy

On July 25 General Carl Spaatz, the U.S. commander in the Pacific, received the order to prepare to use the atomic bomb. The attack would come after August 3, on the first day with weather suitable for the bombing mission. The preferred target was Hiroshima, a city with a population of about 330,000. It was chosen because it had a large military presence, including about 43,000 Japanese troops, supply depots, and factories that made steel and parts for airplanes. Hiroshima had also been largely undamaged by firebombing. U.S. leaders wanted the Japanese to easily see the effects of dropping just a single atomic bomb.

The uranium-gun bomb, Little Boy, reached the Pacific island of Tinian on July 26. By July 31 it was armed and

This photograph captures the destruction caused by the atomic bomb that was dropped on Hiroshima.

ready for use. August 3 was too cloudy for Paul Tibbets and the crew of *Enola Gay* to carry out the mission of dropping the first atomic bomb. The historic day finally came on August 6.

When the bomb exploded, a flash of heat reaching temperatures of 5,400 degrees Fahrenheit swept across Hiroshima. All wood buildings within 1 mile of the center of the blast were destroyed, either by the blast itself or by fire. Stone buildings within one-quarter mile were also demolished.

Hospitals quickly filled with survivors covered with burns. One hospital worker reported seeing patients with no faces: "Theirs eyes, noses, and mouths had been burned away, and it looked like their ears had melted off."

In the Japanese capital of Tokyo government and military leaders received varying reports about what had happened, but President Truman soon made it clear. In a statement read on radio he said, "It is an atomic bomb. It is a harnessing of the basic power of the universe." Truman added that more atomic bombs would be dropped if the Japanese did not surrender.

On August 9 the atomic bomb Fat Man was dropped on the Japanese city of Nagasaki, ending the war with Japan.

Over the next few days no response came from Japan. Emperor Hirohito and others were still not willing to accept an unconditional surrender if that meant no role for the emperor in postwar Japan. Meanwhile, U.S. troops prepared for the second atomic attack, on Nagasaki. A plutonium implosion bomb exploded over that city on August 9. The bomb, called Fat Man, was more powerful than Little Boy, but it landed in a location where the terrain blocked the spread of some heat and radiation. Still, some 40,000 people died that day, and up to 200,000 died in both cities from the effects of the blast and the radiation. The day after the Nagasaki attack the Japanese sent a message to the United States. Japan would accept the Potsdam Declaration, as long as the emperor would have some role in postwar Japan. The United States agreed, and on August 14, 1945, the war with Japan ended.

Six

Reactions and Questions

PRESIDENT HARRY TRUMAN WAS AT SEA, sailing home from Germany, when he heard the news about the successful attack on Hiroshima. "This is the greatest thing in history," he said. Truman's response reflected his hope that the war would soon end. He had no idea of the great number of civilian deaths, and at times he stated his belief that Hiroshima was purely a military target. The Interim Committee Report of May 1945, however, reflects the awareness of U.S. leaders that numerous civilian deaths were likely to follow the dropping of the bomb.

A few days later, after the bombing of Nagasaki, Truman went on the radio and talked about the reasons for the bombings. He explained how the country had been in a race with its enemies to build the first atomic bomb. "Having found the bomb we have used it. We have used it against those who attacked us without warning at Pearl Harbor." Truman added that the Japanese had also carried out cruel acts against U.S. prisoners of war. Finally, he said he had ordered the use of the bomb "to shorten the agony of war, in order to save the lives of thousands and thousands of young Americans."

Awe, Happiness, and Fear

At Los Alamos many of the scientists celebrated when they heard about the bombing of Hiroshima. All their hard work had taken a theory and made it a reality in just over three years. J. Robert Oppenheimer, one scientist later noted, spoke to a cheering crowd of coworkers. The lead scientist for the Manhattan Project "was proud, and he showed it, of what he had accomplished. . . . And his only regret was that we hadn't developed the bomb in time to have used it against the Germans."

On the other hand, some scientists reacted as did Otto Frisch, another Los Alamos collaborator. He watched as some of his coworkers rushed to make reservations at a fancy restaurant, where they could celebrate their achievement. He later wrote how the sight gave him a "feeling of unease, indeed nausea." And one scientist did actually vomit in the bushes after hearing Oppenheimer's speech praising the success of the Manhattan Project.

In the United States newspapers reported the technical breakthrough achieved by the Manhattan Project team (though that code name was not used). *The New York Times* described how the single bomb that hit Hiroshima was equal to all the bombs carried on two thousand B-29s, the bombers that had been used in the previous raids on Japan. The atomic bomb, with the force of around 20,000 tons of TNT, was two thousand times more powerful than any other single bomb before it.

Writing on August 7 for the *Times*, military correspondent Hanson Baldwin said use of the atomic bomb would likely mean a quick victory for the Allies in the Pacific. But greater dangers could lie ahead. Baldwin noted how previous

The New York Times ran a front-page article on the dropping of the atomic bomb on August 7, 1945.

bombings during the war, by both sides, had targeted civilians. "Because our bombing has been more effective and hence more devastating, Americans have become a synonym for destruction. And now we have been the first to introduce a new weapon of unknowable effects which may bring us victory quickly but which will sow the seeds of hate more widely than ever." Other newspapers also feared what the future would bring in the new atomic, or nuclear, age. The *Chicago Tribune* wrote, "It is not impossible that whole cities and all the people in them may be obliterated in a fraction of a second by a single bomb."

Still, some papers and radio reporters stressed the triumph of U.S. science and welcomed the end of the war. So did members of the U.S. military stationed in the Pacific, who feared for their safety if the war dragged on and the Allies invaded Japan. One pilot, John Ciardi, said hearing

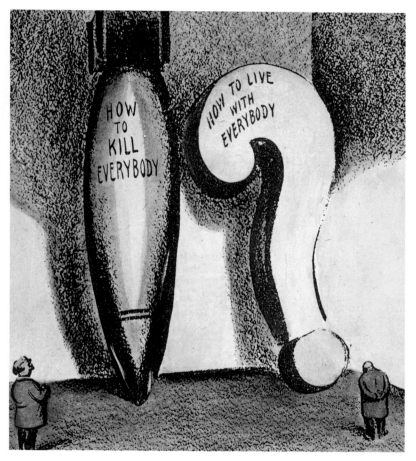

A political cartoon created in 1945 by D. R. Fitzpatrick presents contradictory questions facing the world after the dropping of the atomic bomb.

Public Opinion and the Hiroshima Bombing

The first modern opinion polls were started in the 1930s and were taken to gauge support for political candidates. By the time of the Hiroshima bombing, pollsters were also gathering opinions on important events. In the days after August 6 and 9, one poll found that more than 50 percent of Americans supported the use of the atomic bomb, and 73 percent wished the United States had more of the bombs to use. Another poll said 85 percent favored the bomb's use, with just 10 percent saying it should not have been dropped. Over time, however, the number of Americans who approved of the bombing of Hiroshima fell. In 1995 the number was 44 percent. Opinions may have changed because of the debate since August 1945 over the morality of using nuclear weapons in general and at the end of World War II in particular.

the news about the bombing of Hiroshima was like "we won the lottery. Hey, we're gonna get out of here!" A U.S. soldier later wrote, "When I heard the news, I just got drunk with happiness. . . . My luck would have run out, I am convinced, if I had been a part of the invasion of Japan."

News from Japan

The first news reports out of Japan stressed the horrors of the destruction of Hiroshima and Nagasaki. Not surprisingly, the Japanese sometimes expressed harsh views of the attack, which some writers later called propaganda. An August 8 statement said that the United States would be called "the enemy for ages to come as the destroyer of mankind and as public enemy number 1 of social justice." But one government report stuck to the facts, issuing this description of the aftermath in Hiroshima: "The effect of the bomb is widespread. Those outdoors burned to death, while those indoors were killed by the indescribable pressure and heat."

In the weeks that followed the Japanese also reported the strange illnesses and deaths suffered by survivors of the atomic blasts. Once again some people dismissed this news as propaganda. But in September 1945 a British newspaper published a story called the "Atomic Plague." Its author, the Australian Wilfred Burchett, defied U.S. orders for civilian journalists to stay out of Hiroshima and Nagasaki. The Americans wanted to tightly control the news and images released from the cities.

In his article Burchett said that in Hiroshima, "30 days after the first atomic bomb . . . people are still dying,

mysteriously and horribly . . . from an unknown something."
A little later a *New York Times* reporter allowed into Hiroshima
also noted the deaths of about one hundred people a day.
He described symptoms found by Japanese doctors in the
city: as the survivors' temperatures rose, their white blood
cell counts fell, "their hair began to drop out, they lost their
appetites, vomited blood, and finally died." The victims were
suffering from radiation poisoning, the result of exposure to
high levels of radiation. U.S. scientists had known about this
danger, but they had not predicted that the poisoning would
be so widespread.

The first official news out of Hiroshima came on
September 5. The same day the U.S. government issued
gruesome details of Japanese treatment of Allied prisoners of war—which included chopping off one prisoner's
head and setting other prisoners on fire. *Time* magazine
reported, "The stories, which seemed to have no end,
differed only in the details of calculated cruelty." The
report was perhaps offering a reason why the bomb was
dropped—to end such awful Japanese acts. Or perhaps
it suggested that the American devastation of a city was
a response to Japanese cruelty. In any event the reports
may have influenced the opinion of many Americans that
using the bomb had been the right thing to do.

New Attention on Hiroshima

For months after the end of World War II newspapers and
magazines continued to report on the atomic bomb and its
effects on Japan. But no one story could match the impact
of an article John Hersey wrote for *The New Yorker*, a well-

known weekly magazine. Hersey interviewed six survivors of the Hiroshima bombing and explored the remains of the city. His article filled the entire August 31 issue of the magazine. The issue sold out within hours, and ABC radio later read the article on the air. (The article was later turned into a book, still read today.) Hersey's "Hiroshima" was talked about all over the country. Most people appreciated its straightforward look at the effects of the bombing. Others attacked Hersey for not discussing the bomb's importance in ending the war and saving American lives. Still others disliked the views of some Japanese toward the Americans. Dr. Terufumi Sasaki told Hersey, "I think they ought to try [in court] the men who decided to use the bomb and they should hang them all."

The "Hiroshima" article led some people who once praised the bomb to feel guilty about its use. Manhattan Project scientist A. Squires wrote to a friend, "I wept as I read John Hersey's *New Yorker* account. . . . I am filled with shame to recall the whoopee spirit . . . when we came back from lunch to find others who had returned with the first extras [news] announcing the bombing of Hiroshima." But another reader told *The New Yorker*, "Now let us drop a handful on Moscow." And some people who opposed the use of the bomb thought the article did not truly show its moral horror. Well-known writer Mary McCarthy said Hersey would have had to talk to the people killed at Hiroshima to paint the full picture of its destruction.

As other newspapers and magazines wrote about Hersey's article, James Conant began to worry. Conant, who had been involved with the race to build the bomb from the beginning, did not want the critics of the bomb to have the last word. Even some U.S. military leaders seemed to be questioning the bombing of Hiroshima. Shortly after the "Hiroshima" article appeared, Admiral William Halsey called the atomic bomb a toy that the scientists wanted to try out. "The first atomic bomb," he continued, "was an unnecessary experiment. . . . It was a mistake ever to drop it."

Conant believed the government had to challenge the critical comments emerging about the bomb. He suggested that Henry Stimson write an article explaining why using atomic weapons had been the right thing to do. A small team of writers, including Conant, actually wrote the article, which was titled "The Decision to Use the Atomic Bomb." The article appeared in *Harper's* magazine in February 1947 and was soon reprinted by other magazines and newspapers.

Like Hersey, Stimson suggested that the bomb had saved both Japanese and American lives. Stimson also said that he believed the bombings of Hiroshima and Nagasaki were key in forcing Japan's surrender. He noted too that his and the government's goal was to end the war as quickly as possible with the fewest lives lost. "I believe that no man, in our position and subject to our responsibilities, holding in his hands a weapon of such possibilities for accomplishing this purpose . . . could have failed to use it and afterwards looked his countrymen in the face."

After Stimson's article was published, most of the public debate over Hiroshima's bombing began to fade. Average Americans accepted the government's arguments and the claims by Stimson and others that the United States might

Changing Views over Time

The principal author of the article that appeared in *Harper's* under Henry Stimson's name was McGeorge Bundy, the son of Harvey Bundy, who had been an adviser to Stimson during the war. The younger Bundy used his father's notes while writing the article. He also borrowed ideas from James Conant. Bundy went on to hold key government jobs under two presidents, John F. Kennedy and Lyndon B. Johnson. In 1947 he was proud of the article he wrote, but years later he had slightly changed his views about the use of the atomic bomb. In 1985 he told a television interviewer, "It does seem to me . . . that there were opportunities for communication and warning available to the United States government which were not completely thought through by our government at that time." But Bundy also believed the decision to bomb Hiroshima was a difficult one to make, based on what U.S. leaders knew at the time.

have suffered up to one million American casualties if it had launched a land assault on Japan. But some former government officials who knew about the debates over dropping the bomb, and who thought the war might have ended quickly without it, felt Stimson had not told the complete truth. It would take decades for more facts to emerge.

Seven

Nuclear Arms and the Cold War

THE HERSEY AND STIMSON ARTICLES appeared as the United States was facing new troubles abroad. Since the end of World War II relations between the country and the Soviet Union had worsened. The Soviets increased their efforts to spread communism and dominate governments in Eastern Europe and other areas of the world. President Truman wanted to resist these efforts by sending aid to forces fighting communists. He and his advisers called for a policy of containment—holding communism in where it already existed and stopping its further spread around the world. In a March 1947 speech he said, "The free peoples of the world look to us for support in maintaining their freedoms. If we falter in our leadership, we may endanger the peace of the world—and we shall surely endanger the welfare of our own nation."

This struggle to promote freedom and resist the advances of the Soviet Union was called the cold war. The Soviets and the Americans battled each other by supporting opposing sides in civil wars and revolutions around the world. They sent money, weapons, and supplies to their allies and tried to weaken each other's dominance in certain regions. This struggle went on as the two nations tried to avoid using their armies against each other in a real, "hot" war.

Atomic Rivals

The cold war unfolded under the shadow of Hiroshima and the reality of nuclear weapons. Even before August 6, 1945, some U.S. leaders had called for sharing information with the Soviets about the bomb. They saw this as a way to win Joseph Stalin's trust and ensure peace between the two powerful nations. Along with sharing technical data on how to make a bomb, the United States could push for international control of atomic weapons.

After the bombing of Hiroshima, Henry Stimson suggested that the Americans share nuclear knowledge with the Soviets only as long as the Soviets did not try to build a bomb and made peaceful use of the information. Secretary of State James Byrnes and other advisers, however, opposed any kind of arrangement with the Soviet Union. Some U.S. military planners were even considering the possible use of atomic weapons against the Soviet Union or any other "aggressor nation" that seemed close to getting its own nuclear weapons. Atomic bombs could also be used against the Soviets if they launched an attack with nonatomic weapons.

In late 1945 most of the Manhattan Project scientists believed that scientists in the Soviet Union would soon be able to build their own bomb. What they didn't know until several years later was that Soviet spies had worked on the Manhattan Project. They had collected information on using the implosion method to make an atomic bomb. The Soviet

Union used this information to build its own bomb, which was secretly tested in August 1949.

In the weeks that followed U.S. sensors found radioactive evidence of the test blast. Truman knew that the United States was no longer the world's only nuclear

The New York paper *The Sun* announces Russia's detonation of an atomic bomb in 1949.

Cold War Fears

During World War II General Leslie Groves said he always thought Soviet spies were a greater danger to the United States than German ones. The extent of the Soviet espionage done at Los Alamos seemed to support this. The U.S. government first got some indication of the spying through a secret program called Venona. The Americans intercepted messages sent between Soviet officials in Moscow and their representatives in the United States, then broke the code in which they were sent. Further proof came in 1950 with the arrest of Klaus Fuchs, one of the spies mentioned in the Venona messages. Other spies were arrested, and Senator Joseph McCarthy announced that various U.S. government agencies were still filled with spies. That charge was not true, but the cold war, the capture of the Los Alamos spies, and the Soviet Union's successful test of atomic weapons led to an atmosphere of fear. Laws were passed calling on teachers and other public figures to take loyalty oaths, and anyone with connections to socialist or communist groups was considered a possible traitor. This "McCarthy era" is still hotly debated by historians. Some think the country had a real reason to fear Soviet influence in the United States; others, however, see an overreaction that led to unfair limits being placed on the rights of U.S. citizens.

power. And the scientific evidence, as well as later Soviet statements, showed that the Soviet scientists had improved on the design of the bomb used at Hiroshima. The Soviet atomic bomb posed a new threat to U.S. security. The two countries then began a race to build more and bigger nuclear weapons than the other and to devise better ways to deliver them to enemy targets.

Going Super

Truman took the first step in this arms race by approving a project to build the "superbomb"—a fusion bomb based on hydrogen, the most common element in the universe. The H-bomb, as it was also called, promised to cause even more destruction than the weapon dropped on Hiroshima.

The call for building the hydrogen bomb had actually started in 1946, led primarily by Edward Teller, who had worked on the Manhattan Project. Many scientists spoke out against the new bomb, fearing its awesome power. A committee within the Atomic Energy Commission, which had been created in 1946, opposed building the superbomb. Its members include J. Robert Oppenheimer and James Conant. In a report the committee issued in October 1949, Enrico Fermi and Isidor Rabi added a separate statement of their personal beliefs: "It is clear that the use of such a weapon cannot be justified on any ethical ground. . . . It is necessarily an evil thing considered in any light." They added that atomic bombs offered the United States everything it needed to protect itself.

But in the cold war atmosphere military leaders and Truman believed they could not risk letting the Soviet Union develop the superbomb first. The military especially was concerned that the Soviets would do anything to achieve world domination. In January 1950 Truman told Congress and the American people that work would begin on the superbomb, and the Soviet Union immediately began its own H-bomb project. Just as in World War II a scientific and military race was on.

Success and Tragedy

By November 1952 the United States was ready to test its first hydrogen bomb. The test took place in the Marshall Islands, in the Pacific Ocean. The blast was one thousand times more powerful than the bomb used on Hiroshima, and it created a crater 1 mile wide and 200 feet deep. Harold Agnew was

One of the largest nuclear blasts in the Pacific Ocean was Ivy Mike, which destroyed Elugelab Island.

Horror on Film

In the months after the deadly H-bomb test, Japanese moviegoers got their first look at a new film monster— Godzilla. In the film, called *Gojira*, Godzilla is stirred from his home deep under the Pacific by a nuclear weapons test. The giant reptile then attacks Tokyo, destroying buildings and people with fire that shoots from its mouth. U.S. filmmakers had already made several movies with monsters that were created by radiation from atomic tests. Godzilla, however, had a strong impact on the Japanese, with their direct experience of the horrors of nuclear weapons and radiation. A version of *Gojira* was released in the United States in 1956. Called *Godzilla, King of the Monsters*, the film cut from the Japanese original all mentions of Hiroshima and Nagasaki, as well as most references to atomic weapons.

a scientist who watched the test. He later recalled, "You don't know what heat is until you've seen the heat from a . . . hydrogen bomb. It doesn't stop, it just gets hotter and hotter and you start to really worry even though you're 20-some miles away."

The United States continued to test hydrogen bombs in remote parts of the Pacific. Officials warned boats to stay out of the test areas, so they would not pass under drifting clouds of radioactive dust and ash, called fallout. But during a March 1954 test the size of the blast was bigger than the Americans expected, and the fallout covered a much greater area.

Some 85 miles away fishers onboard the Japanese ship *Fukuryu Maru* (Lucky Dragon) saw the bomb test. Within several hours radioactive fallout began to rain down on the ship. Soon, all twenty-three men on the *Fukuryu Maru* became sick. One later died from a kidney problem related to radiation poisoning. In Japan the *Fukuryu Maru* incident stirred up memories of Hiroshima and anger toward the United States. One Japanese newspaper wrote, "Once again the Japanese have been poisoned by ashes of death." The fish the sailors had caught were also poisoned by the fallout, and for months most Japanese stopped eating all fish. The Japanese also began to protest U.S. nuclear testing in the Pacific, with 32 million signing a petition calling for the tests to end.

Just after the *Fukuryu Maru* tragedy unfolded, memories of Hiroshima were brought to the forefront in the United States. In May 1955 a group of women who had been hurt during the Hiroshima bombing arrived in New York. These twenty-five women were known as the Hiroshima Maidens, and they were just some of the *hibakusha* — "explosion-affected people" — who survived the atomic bombings but were left badly scarred or disfigured. An American newspaper editor, some U.S. Quakers, and two surgeons worked together to bring the women to America, where they could receive plastic surgery for their scars.

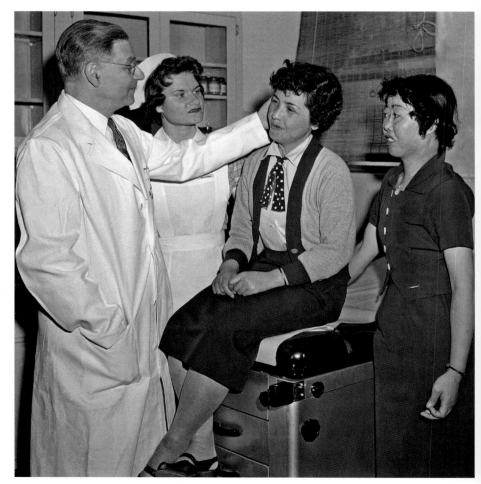

Two "Hiroshima Maidens" undergo an exam at Mount Sinai Hospital in New York City in May 1955.

At first the U.S. government tried to prevent the arrival of the young women—it did not want to seem to be admitting any moral wrongdoing for the bombing. Some officials also feared that seeing the victims of an atomic attack would spur some Americans to support efforts to outlaw nuclear weapons. This movement was just beginning to arise in Japan and other parts of the world. The State Department tried to cancel the flight carrying the women to the United States, but it had already left Japan. When the women arrived, the government would not let pictures or television images of them be shown. Several of the women appeared on the TV show *This Is Your Life* but had to stand behind a curtain so viewers could see only outlines of their bodies.

The Hiroshima Maidens received a warm welcome and gratefully accepted donations from Americans to pay for their trip. But the unease of U.S. government officials suggested their awareness that nuclear weapons were always bound to stir controversy, especially as the country continued to add them to its arsenal.

Eight

An Enduring Debate

As THE COLD WAR WENT ON THROUGHOUT THE 1950s and beyond, the United States and the Soviet Union built more and larger nuclear weapons. They perfected better ways of delivering those weapons to potential targets, with rockets that could carry nuclear warheads thousands of miles in mere minutes. At times the world watched with fear when tensions between the two countries rose and it seemed possible that one side might launch a nuclear attack on the other.

By the 1960s, however, Soviet and U.S. leaders knew that launching a first strike with nuclear weapons would lead to the other side returning fire with its own deadly barrage. This idea of "mutually assured destruction" (MAD) led the two countries to try to find peaceful solutions to their problems. Still, the threat of a nuclear attack remained real, and many also worried about the accidental launch of a rocket loaded with an H-bomb. The era that began with Hiroshima had created a new and frightening reality. In the words of historian Martin Sherwin, the use of atomic weapons in Japan raised a crucial idea: "The survival of humanity could no longer be assumed."

Staying Safe?

At various times during the cold war both the Soviet Union and the United States taught its citizens what to do in case of a nuclear attack. In the United States these civil defense programs included building bomb shelters. The shelters were stocked with food and were supposed to keep people safe until the fallout from a nuclear blast had passed. In schools many children were taught to duck under their desks and cover their heads with their hands. In the event of a nuclear war the civil defense programs probably would not have saved many lives, but they gave citizens a sense of security, which lessened their fears. If an all-out nuclear attack had occurred during the cold war, millions of people would have died.

Exploring Hiroshima over Time

During those decades of nuclear uncertainty scholars looked back to the start of the nuclear era, the bombing of Hiroshima and Nagasaki. Many were especially concerned by Truman's decision to drop the first atomic bombs and were not persuaded by the official explanations. Most Americans, however, accepted the reasoning of Henry Stimson in the 1947 *Harper's* article. Dropping the bomb was necessary to end the war quickly and save lives. Few people seemed to notice or think much about the military leaders and scientists who challenged this view in 1945 and thereafter.

The first scholarly book to examine the decision to use the bomb appeared in 1961. Herbert Feis had worked in the U.S. State Department before taking this historical look at the decision. In *Japan Subdued: The Atomic Bomb and the End of the War in the Pacific*, Feis said that Truman had decided to bomb Hiroshima for the military reasons usually given — to end the war as soon as possible. But Feis also cited evidence showing that some U.S. military leaders believed the war with Japan would have ended in 1945 even without the bombs — and without an Allied invasion of Japan. He suggested, as scientists and others had done in 1945, that the United States could have warned the Japanese about the power of the new bomb it had developed.

Four years later Gar Alperovitz published a book called *Atomic Diplomacy*. Alperovitz suggested that diplomatic concerns — trying to influence Soviet behavior in Europe — played the largest part in the decision to bomb Hiroshima. He also said that more evidence would need to come out of government files to prove or disprove this idea. That evidence would continue to emerge over the next several decades, and several other historians tackled the issue of why the United States bombed Hiroshima. Most, as J. Samuel Walker wrote in *Prompt and Utter Destruction*, rejected "the traditional view that the bomb was the only alternative to an invasion of Japan." Truman and his advisers could have continued firebombings or tightened their blockade and still ended the war by 1946. Walker said that most historians seemed to believe that military considerations were the main factor in Truman's decision to use the bomb, but they saw that foreign policy—postwar relations with the Soviets—also played a part.

A few historians also suggested that racism influenced Truman's decision. One was Ronald Takaki. In *Hiroshima: Why America Dropped the Bomb*, published in 1995, Takaki argued that Truman, like many Americans at the time, had racist views of the Japanese. Newspapers often referred to the Japanese as "Japs" and used other insulting words to describe them. On a float used during a 1942 parade in New York City, the Japanese were shown as rats. In one letter written after the Hiroshima bombing, Truman wrote, "When you have to deal with a beast you have to treat him as a beast." But Truman's defenders said he was responding to the brutal tactics the Japanese were using during the war more than displaying a racist bent. They also pointed out that the United States had begun the Manhattan Project planning to use atomic weapons against Germany. If the bombs had been ready before Germany's surrender, they might have been used on German targets. Still, Takaki believed the Americans were more willing to use the atomic bombs on Japan because of racist attitudes toward the Japanese people.

Alperovitz, Takaki, and other critics of Truman's decision have been called revisionist historians. Some historians say they manipulate the facts to present their own views, often to cast Truman and his advisers in a negative light. Historians who accept the more traditional view of the decision, as laid out by Truman and Stimson, have tried to refute the revisionists. They include Robert James Maddox, author of *Weapons for Victory: The Hiroshima Decision Fifty Years Later*. Maddox wrote that "Truman was commander in chief of American armed forces and had a duty to the men under his command. . . . One can only imagine what would have happened had tens of thousands of young Americans been killed or wounded on Japanese soil, and then it became known that the president had chosen not to employ weapons that might have ended the war months earlier." Maddox also said there is no evidence that any of the military leaders who later condemned the bombing of Hiroshima expressed their feelings to Truman before the bomb was used.

The *Enola Gay* Controversy

Maddox, Takaki, Alperovitz, and others published books about Hiroshima in 1995—the fiftieth anniversary of the dropping of the atomic bomb. That anniversary year also saw the opening of an exhibit at the Smithsonian Institution in Washington, D.C. For decades the Smithsonian's Air and Space Museum had stored the *Enola Gay*, the plane used to drop the first atomic bomb. During the 1980s some military veterans called on the museum to restore and display the historic plane, and the Smithsonian agreed.

An exhibit called "The Last Act: The Atomic Bomb and the End of World War II," was scheduled to open in 1995. It would feature the *Enola Gay* and would explain the decision to use the atomic bomb on Hiroshima. But as the exhibit was developed, a heated public debate erupted. Military veterans wanted the plane featured on its own, to recognize the bravery and patriotism of Paul Tibbets and the others who carried out the historic mission over Hiroshima. They disliked the Smithsonian's idea of putting the plane in a larger exhibit about the atomic bomb—and one that seemed to reflect the revisionist thinking on why the bomb was used.

The veterans' concerns led them to contact members of Congress and the media. By the summer of 1994 the Smithsonian was facing pressure to change its plans for the exhibit. Critics felt it placed too much emphasis on the destruction caused by the bombing while ignoring the many Japanese acts of brutality throughout the war. One letter from several dozen lawmakers said they were concerned that in the proposed exhibit, Japan was "portrayed more as an innocent victim . . . and . . . Americans as being driven to drop the bomb out of revenge and for political reasons."

The director of the museum, Martin Harwit, thought the lawmakers and veterans were ignoring evidence historians had uncovered since 1945. Still, the Smithsonian agreed to cancel its planned exhibit. The *Enola Gay* went on display in 1995, but the material presented focused on the plane and the men who flew it. Nothing was said about the decision to drop the bomb or the effects of that action. The exhibit originally planned, Harwit later wrote, offended some Americans who did not want to "cast into doubt a . . . patriotic story . . . of America's sacrifices and ultimate victory in World War II."

In 1995 Americans were not the only ones who disagreed about Hiroshima and what it meant. In Japan, some people still condemned the attack. Hitoshi Motoshima served as mayor of Nagasaki during the 1980s and 1990s. He said in 1995, "I think the atomic bombings were one of the two greatest crimes against humanity in the 20th century, along with the Holocaust." But Shizuko Abe, a survivor of the Hiroshima blast, had a different view. "I've never had a grudge against the United States. Japan also did lots of things in the war. The bomb didn't drop out of the blue. It happened in the process of war."

Hiroshima and Nuclear Weapons Today

New books continue to appear about Hiroshima. Historians continue to debate the possibility that the war could have been ended quickly without the use of atomic weapons. Some say Russia's entry into the war would have forced Japan's surrender without using the bombs. Others argue the Japanese government was ready to fight on, despite the suffering it was enduring. The scholars look for new evidence, hoping to answer once and for all the questions surrounding the dropping of the bomb. The questions of historical fact—who did what, when, and why—are tied to moral questions. Was it right to drop the bomb and kill so many civilians? Should the Americans have seen that they would begin

The Future of Nuclear Weapons

As some people work to eliminate all nuclear weapons, the government of the United States continues to consider them a legitimate option during war. Starting in 2002 President George W. Bush called for the development of new hydrogen bombs, having already said that the United States had the right to use nuclear weapons against countries that did not have them, if the other countries threatened U.S. security. Even with the end of the cold war the United States retains several thousand nuclear warheads. In 2007 a group of retired government leaders—including Secretaries of State Henry Kissinger and George Shultz—called for new efforts to stop the spread of nuclear weapons and to reduce existing arsenals. They wrote, "Reassertion of the vision of a world free of nuclear weapons . . . would be perceived as . . . a bold initiative consistent with America's moral heritage."

a nuclear arms race that would lead to the creation of thousands of bombs able to kill millions of people?

Although the cold war ended in 1991, the world still faces the risk of nuclear attacks. About ten countries have nuclear weapons or are trying to build them. A few nations say they simply want to use nuclear power to generate electricity. But acquiring the technology for the peaceful use of nuclear fission can also be the first step toward making potent weapons. And some experts fear these weapons could end up in the

A technician dismantles a thermonuclear warhead in France in 1998.

hands of terrorists who would not hesitate to use violence to achieve their political goals.

Japan, because of its experiences in World War II, was the home of the first major effort to eliminate nuclear weapons. Today, hundreds of organizations around the world have that goal. Their members fear what would happen if nuclear weapons, now so much more powerful than the one dropped on Hiroshima, were ever used again.

Timeline

1931   Japan seizes Manchuria, China.

1933   Adolf Hitler and the Nazi Party come to power in Germany.

1937   Japan forcibly extends its control over more of China.

1938   German scientists Otto Hahn and Fritz Strassmann split atoms of uranium.

1939   Albert Einstein sends a letter to President Franklin Roosevelt explaining the significance of research in nuclear fission; Germany invades Poland, beginning World War II; Uranium Committee meets for the first time to discuss nuclear research.

1941   U.S. officials read the MAUD Report, which suggests that atomic bombs can be built; Japan attacks Pearl Harbor, bringing the United States into World War II.

1942   U.S. atomic research program is named the Manhattan Project; scientists at the University of Chicago achieve the first sustained nuclear fission chain reaction.

1943   Work on building an atomic bomb begins in Los Alamos, New Mexico.

1945   Franklin Roosevelt dies, and Harry Truman becomes president; Germany surrenders, but fighting continues in the Pacific against Japan; first test of an atomic bomb occurs near Alamogordo, New Mexico; Allies issue the Potsdam Declaration, calling for Japan's unconditional surrender, and Japan refuses; President Truman decides to use the atomic bomb against Japan; atomic bombs are dropped on Hiroshima and Nagasaki; Japan surrenders.

1946 *The New Yorker* publishes John Hersey's article on Hiroshima.

1947 *Harper's* publishes Secretary of War Henry L. Stimson's explanation of why the atomic bomb was dropped on Hiroshima.

1949 The Soviet Union tests its first atomic bomb.

1950 President Truman announces his decision to develop a hydrogen "superbomb" based on nuclear fusion.

1952 The United States tests the first hydrogen bomb.

1954 The test of a hydrogen bomb sickens Japanese fishers near the test site; one later dies from radiation poisoning.

1955 "Hiroshima Maidens"—young women badly injured during the 1945 bombing—come to the United States for reconstructive surgery.

1994 After public controversy, the Smithsonian Institution cancels a planned exhibit on the bombing of Hiroshima.

Notes

Introduction

p. 7, "Now I am become Death, the destroyer of worlds": J. Robert Oppenheimer, quoted in "The Trinity Test," The Manhattan Project: An Interactive History. Office of Heritage and History Resources, U.S. Department of Energy. http://www.cfo.doe. gov/me70/manhattan/trinity.htm (Accessed 14 April 2008).

Chapter One

p. 9, "You know what . . . special": Paul Tibbets, quoted in "Nuclear Special: 'One Hell of a Big Bang.'" *The Guardian*, 6 August 2002. Online at Guardian.co.uk. http://www.guardian.co.uk/world/2002/aug/06/nuclear.japan (Accessed 22 February 2008).

p. 13, "Miss Yamaoka, you look like a monster": Unnamed friend, quoted in Richard B. Frank, *Downfall: The End of the Imperial Japanese Empire*. New York: Penguin Books, 1999, p. 265.

p. 14, "All we saw . . . something like this": Theodore "Dutch" J. Van Kirk, quoted in "Young Men and Bombs," *Time*, 23 July 2005. http://www.time.com/time/world/article/0,8599,1086088,00. html (Accessed 22 February 2008).

p. 15, "A massive cloud . . . out into the streets": Toyofumi Ogura, *Letters from the End of the World: A Firsthand Account of the Bombing of Hiroshima*. Translated by Kisaburo Murakami and Shigeru Fujii. New York: Kodansha International, 1997, p. 17.

Chapter Two

p. 17, "I pledge you, I pledge myself, to a new deal for the American people": Franklin Roosevelt, *Great Speeches*. John Grafton, ed. Mineola, NY: Dover, 1999, p. 17.

p. 19, "The next five years . . . German people": Adolf Hitler, quoted in Piers Brendon, *The Dark Valley: A Panorama of the 1930s*. New York: Knopf, 2000, p. 281.

p. 22, "never be allowed to return to Chinese hands": Sadao Araki, quoted in Brendon, *The Dark Valley*, p. 223.

p. 23, "in the hands of virtually mad dogs": Henry L. Stimson, quoted in Thomas G. Paterson, J. Garry Clifford, and Kenneth J. Hagan, *American Foreign Relations: A History Since 1895*, vol. II. Boston: Houghton Mifflin, 2000, p. 144.

p. 23, "growing ill-will . . . general war": Franklin D. Roosevelt, quoted in Kenneth S. Davis, *FDR: The New Deal Years, 1933–1937*. New York: Random House, 1986, p. 593.

p. 24, "war and preparation . . . profit for the few": Gerald Nye, "Merchants of Death," Historical Minute Essays. United States Senate. http://www.senate.gov/artand history/history /minute/merchants_of_death.htm (Accessed 15 April 2008).

p. 25, "internal affairs . . . our desires": Charles A. Lindbergh, "Our Relationship with Europe." Charles A. Lindbergh: An American Aviator. http://www.charleslindbergh.com/ americanfirst/speech3.asp (Accessed 15 April 2008).

p. 26, "the peace . . . international order and law": Roosevelt, *Great Speeches*, p. 66.

p. 28, "Japan had already set . . . agreed to her demands": Henry L. Stimson, quoted in Robert Dallek, *Franklin D. Roosevelt and American Foreign Policy, 1932–1945*. New York: Oxford University Press, 1979, p. 306.

p. 29, "I have directed . . . absolute victory": Roosevelt, *Great Speeches*, p. 115.

Chapter Three

p. 30, "that very small amounts . . . and vice versa": Albert Einstein, "Einstein Explains the Equivalence of Energy and Matter," A. Einstein: Image and Impact. American Institute of Physics Center for the History of Physics. http://www.aip.org/history/einstein/voice1.htm (Accessed 16 April 2008).

p. 32, "carried by boat . . . surrounding territory": Albert Einstein, letter to Franklin D. Roosevelt, 2 August 1939. Argonne National Laboratory. http://www.anl.gov/Science_and_Technology/History/Anniversary_Frontiers/aetofdr.html (Accessed 17 April 2008).

p. 34, "If I had known . . . lifted a finger": Albert Einstein, quoted in "The Uranium Committee," Manhattan Project History: Early Government Support. The Atomic Heritage Foundation. http://www.atomicheritage.org/index.php?option=com_content&task=view&id=174&Itemid=118 (Accessed on 17 April 2008).

p. 38, "equivalent . . . human life for a long period": The MAUD Report, Nuclear Files.org. The Nuclear Age Peace Foundation. http://www.nuclearfiles.org/menu/key-issues/nuclear-weapons/history/pre-cold-war/manhattan-project/maud-report.htm (Accessed 17 April 2008).

p. 38, "Time . . . is very much of the essence." Franklin D. Roosevelt, quoted in Martin J. Sherwin, *A World Destroyed: Hiroshima and Its Legacies*, 3rd ed. Stanford, CA: Stanford University Press, 2003, p. 39.

p. 41, "The Italian navigator has just landed in the New World": Arthur Compton, quoted in "The Chain Reaction: December 2, 1942 and After." The Special Collections Research Center, the University of Chicago Library. http://

www.lib.uchicago.edu/e/spcl/chain.html#b (Accessed 18 April 2008).

p. 41, "black day in the history of mankind": Leo Szilard, quoted in "CP-1 Goes Critical," The Manhattan Project: An Interactive History. Office of Heritage and History Resources, U.S. Department of Energy. http://www.cfo.doe.gov/me70/manhattan/cp-1_critical.htm (Accessed 18 April 2008).

Chapter Four

p. 42, "eager to show this loyalty": Curtis Munson, "Japanese on the West Coast," quoted in Greg Robinson, *By Order of the President: FDR and the Internment of Japanese Americans*. Cambridge, MA: Harvard University Press, 2001, p. 67.

p. 43, "A viper . . . not an American." *Los Angeles Times*, quoted in J. Burton et al., *Confinement and Ethnicity: An Overview of World War II Japanese American Relocation Sites*. Online at the National Parks Service. http://www.nps.gov/history/history/online_books/anthropology74/ce3c.htm (Accessed 19 April 2008.)

p. 46, "Although their removal . . . least possible hardship": "The Best Way to Show Loyalty," *San Francisco News*, 6 March 1942. Virtual Museum of the City of San Francisco. http://www.sfmuseum.org/hist8/editorial1.html (Accessed 19 April 2008).

p. 47, "The stall . . . constantly hungry": Yoshiko Uchida, *Desert Exile*, excerpted in *Only What We Could Carry: The Japanese Internment Experience*, Lawson Fusao Inada, ed. Berkeley, CA: Heyday Books, 2000, pp. 71, 73.

p. 51, "when a 'bomb' . . . the Japanese.": Franklin D. Roosevelt and Winston Churchill, Aide-mémoire of 18 September 1944, reprinted in Sherwin, *A World Destroyed*, p. 284.

p. 52, "a most urgent matter": Henry L. Stimson, quoted in J. Samuel Walker, *Prompt and Utter Destruction: Truman and the Use of Atomic Bombs Against Japan.* Rev. ed. Chapel Hill: University of North Carolina Press, 2004, p. 13.

p. 52, "Within four months . . . destroy a whole city": Henry L. Stimson, quoted in David McCullough, *Truman.* New York: Simon & Schuster, 1992, p. 377.

Chapter Five

p. 55, "Gentlemen . . . the course of civilization": Henry L. Stimson, quoted in McCullough, *Truman*, p. 390.

p. 56, "At this stage . . . in that sense": Thomas Searle, quoted in Joseph Coleman, "1945 Tokyo Firebombing Left Legacy of Terror, Pain." Online at Common Dreams.org News Center. http://www.commondreams.org/headlines05/0310-08.htm (Accessed 26 April 2008).

p. 58, "range from . . . to induce surrender": J. Robert Oppenheimer et al., "Recommendations on the Immediate Use of Nuclear Weapons," reprinted in Sherwin, *A World Destroyed*, pp. 304–305.

p. 58, "direct military use": in Sherwin, *A World Destroyed*, pp. 304–305.

p. 59, "with reluctance . . . bomb on Japan": James Byrnes, quoted in McCullough, *Truman*, p. 391.

p. 60, "it may be very difficult . . . international agreement": James Franck, quoted in Sherwin, *A World Destroyed*, p. 211.

p. 61, "The position . . . for this feeling." Ralph Bard, "Memorandum on the Use of the S-1 Bomb," Nuclear Files.org. The Nuclear

Age Peace Foundation. http://www.nuclearfiles.org/menu/library/correspondence/bard-ralph/corr_bard_1945-06-27.htm (Accessed 28 April 2008).

p. 61, "It was a great new force . . . never for evil": Thomas Farrell, "War Department Release on New Mexico Test, July 16, 1945," reprinted at Trinity Atomic website. http://www.cddc.vt.edu/host/atomic/trinity/wd_press.html (Accessed 29 April 2008).

p. 63, "We call upon . . . prompt and utter destruction": Potsdam Declaration, reprinted at Birth of the Constitution of Japan. http://www.ndl.go.jp/constitution/e/etc/c06.html (Accessed 29 April 2008).

p. 64, "We are now . . . at home and abroad": Shigenori Togo, quoted in Frank, *Downfall*, p. 222.

p. 67, "Their eyes . . . had melted off": Katsutani [no first name given], quoted in Frank, *Downfall*, p. 267.

p. 68, "It is an atomic bomb . . . universe": Harry S. Truman, "Statement by the President Announcing the Use of the A-Bomb at Hiroshima." Harry S. Truman Library and Museum. http://www.trumanlibrary.org/calendar/viewpapers.php?pid=100 (Accessed 1 May 2008).

Chapter Six

p. 70, "This is the greatest thing in history": Harry S. Truman, quoted in McCullough, *Truman*, p. 454.

p. 70, "Having found the bomb . . . to shorten the agony . . . thousands of young Americans." quoted in McCullough, *Truman*, p. 459.

p. 71, "was proud . . . against the Germans": Unnamed scientist, quoted in *Eye-Witness Hiroshima*, Adrian Weale, ed. New York: Carroll & Graf, 1995, p. 174.

p. 71, "feeling of unease, indeed nausea": Otto Frisch, quoted in *Eye-Witness Hiroshima*, Weale, ed., p. 173.

p. 72, "Because our bombing . . . more widely than ever": Hanson W. Baldwin, "The Atomic Weapon: End of War Against Japan Hastened But Destruction Sows Seed of Hate," *New York Times*, 7 August 1945, p. 10.

p. 72, "It is not impossible . . . a single bomb": *Chicago Tribune*, quoted in McCullough, *Truman*, p. 456.

p. 75, "we won . . . get out of here!" John Ciardi, quoted in Robert Jay Lifton and Greg Mitchell, *Hiroshima in America: A Half Century of Denial*. New York: Avon Books, 1995, p. 33.

p. 75, "when I heard the news . . . invasion of Japan": Unnamed soldier, quoted in Gar Alperovitz, *The Decision to Use the Atomic Bomb*. New York: Alfred A. Knopf, 1995, p. 423.

p. 75, "enemy for ages . . . social justice": Japanese government radio statement, quoted in Weale, ed., *Eye-Witness Hiroshima*, p. 175.

p. 75, "The effect . . . pressure and heat": quoted in Weale, ed., *Eye-Witness Hiroshima*, p. 175.

p. 75, "30 days after . . . an unknown something": Wilfred Burchett, quoted in Lifton and Mitchell, *Hiroshima in America*, p. 47.

p. 76, "their hair began . . . finally died": W. H. Lawrence, "Visit to Hiroshima Proves It World's Most-Damaged City," *The New York Times*, 5 September 1945, pp. 1, 4.

p. 76, "The stories . . . calculated cruelty": "Before Hiroshima," *Time*, 17 September 1945. Online at Time.com, http://www.time.com/time/magazine/article/0,9171,854438,00.html?promoid=googlep (Accessed 12 May 2008).

p. 77, "I think . . . hang them all." Terufumi Sasaki, quoted in John Hersey, *Hiroshima*. New ed. New York: Knopf, 1985, p. 117.

p. 77, "I am filled . . . the bombing of Hiroshima." A. Squires, quoted in Steve Rothman, "The Publication of 'Hiroshima' in *The New Yorker.*" http://www.herseyhiroshima.com/index.php (Accessed 12 May 2008).

p. 77, "Now let us drop a handful on Moscow." Unnamed reader, quoted in Lifton and Mitchell, *Hiroshima in America*, pp. 88–89.

p. 78, "The first atomic bomb . . . mistake ever to drop it": William Halsey, quoted in Alperovitz, *The Decision to Use the Atomic Bomb*, p. 445.

p. 78, "I believe that no man . . . looked his countrymen in the face": Henry L. Stimson, quoted in William L. Laurence, "Stimson Reveals Story of Atom Use," *New York Times*, 28 January 1947, p. 1.

p. 79, "It does seem to me . . . at that time": McGeorge Bundy, quoted in Benina Berger Gould, *Living in the Question? The Berlin Nuclear Crisis Critical Oral History, Part II*. Berkeley: University of California Institute of Slavic, East European, and Eurasian Studies, 2004. Online at http://repositories.cdlib.org/cgi/viewcontent.cgi?article=1002&context=iseees (Accessed 13 May 2008).

Chapter Seven

p. 81, "The free peoples . . . of our own nation": Harry S. Truman, "Address Before a Joint Session of Congress, March 12, 1947," the Avalon Project. http://www.yale.edu/lawweb/avalon/trudoc.htm (Accessed 14 May 2008).

p. 86, "It is clear . . . in any light": Enrico Fermi and Isidor

Rabi, "An Opinion on the Development of the 'Super,'" General Advisory Committee's Majority and Minority Reports on Building the H-Bomb. *Race for the Superbomb*, The American Experience. http://www.pbs.org/wgbh/amex/bomb/filmmore/reference/primary/extractsofgeneral.html (Accessed 14 May 2008).

p. 89, "You don't know . . . 20-some miles away": Harold Agnew, "Sputnik," *Cold War*. CNN Interactive. http://www.cnn.com/SPECIALS/cold.war/episodes/08/script.html (Accessed 15 May 2008).

p. 89, "Once again the Japanese have been poisoned by ashes of death": Unnamed Tokyo paper, quoted in Agnew, "Sputnik."

Chapter Eight

p. 92, "The survival of humanity could no longer be assumed": Sherwin, *A World Destroyed*, p. 3.

p. 95, "traditional view . . . invasion of Japan": Walker, *Prompt and Utter Destruction*, p. 106.

p. 95, "When you have to deal . . . a beast": Harry S. Truman, letter to Samuel McCrea Cavert, 11 August 1945. Nuclear Files.Org. The Nuclear Age Peace Foundation. http://www.nuclearfiles.org/menu/library/correspondence/truman-harry/corr_truman_1945-08-11.htm (Accessed 1 June 2008).

p. 96, "Truman was commander . . . months earlier": Robert J. Maddox, quoted in James E. Auer and Richard Halloran, "Looking Back at the Bomb." *Parameters*, Spring 1996. U.S. Army War College Quarterly. http://www.carlisle.army.

mil/USAWC/parameters/96spring/sp-essay.htm (Accessed on June 1, 2008).

p. 97, "portrayed more . . . for political reasons": Peter Blute and 23 other members of the U.S. House of Representatives, letter to Secretary Robert McCormick Adams, 10 August 1994. Quoted in Martin Harwit, *An Exhibit Denied: Lobbying the History of the* Enola Gay. New York: Copernicus, 1996, p. 257.

p. 98, "cast into doubt . . . ultimate victory in World War II": Harwit, *An Exhibit Denied*, pp. 426–427.

p. 98, "I think . . . along with the Holocaust": Hitoshi Motoshima, quoted in Nicholas D. Kristof, "Hiroshima: A Special Report; The Bomb: An Act That Haunts Japan and America," *New York Times*, 6 August 1995. Online at NYTimes.com. http://query.nytimes.com/gst/fullpage.html ?res=990CE0D91430F935A3575BC0A963958260. (Accessed 18 May 2008).

p. 98, "I've never had . . . the process of war": Shizuko Abe, quoted in Kristoff, "Hiroshima: A Special Report."

p. 99, "Reassertion of the vision . . . America's moral heritage": Henry Kissinger et al, "World Free of Nuclear Weapons," *Wall Street Journal*, 4 January 2007, p. A15. Reprinted in *The Manhattan Project*, Cynthia C. Kelly, ed. New York: Black Dog & Leventhal Publishers, 2007, p. 452.

Further Information

Books

Allman, Toney. *J. Robert Oppenheimer: Theoretical Physicist, Atomic Pioneer.* Detroit: Blackbirch Press, 2005.

Langley, Andrew. *Hiroshima and Nagasaki: Fire from the Sky.* Minneapolis: Compass Point Books, 2006.

Orr, Tamra. *The Atom Bomb: Creating and Exploding the First Nuclear Weapon.* New York: Rosen Publishing Group, 2005.

Otfinoski, Steven. *Harry S. Truman: America's 33rd President.* Danbury, CT: Children's Press, 2005.

Sheehan, Sean. *World War II: The Pacific.* Milwaukee: World Almanac Library, 2005.

Sirimarco, Elizabeth. *The Cold War.* New York: Benchmark Books, 2005.

Yeatts, Tabatha. *Albert Einstein: The Miracle Mind.* New York: Sterling, 2007.

Video/DVDs

Enola Gay. A & E Home Video, 2005.

White Light, Black Rain: The Destruction of Hiroshima and Nagasaki. HBO Video, 2007.

Websites

The Manhattan Project: An Interactive History
www.cfo.doe.gov/me70/manhattan/index.htm
This website from the U.S. Department of Energy offers a detailed look at the development of the atomic bomb, going back to important scientific discoveries of the late nineteenth

century. The site also has photos of many of the people and places that were part of the Manhattan Project.

The Atomic Heritage Foundation
www.atomicheritage.org
This site is dedicated to the history of the Manhattan Project, with interactive maps and primary source documents. The site also has a section on the women of the Manhattan Project.

Harry S. Truman Library
www.trumanlibrary.org
The official online source for President Truman's papers has copies of important documents connected with the decision to bomb Hiroshima. These include letters and notes from meetings. The site also includes an entire book about Truman and his decision to use the atomic bomb.

The *Enola Gay* Controversy
digital.lib.lehigh.edu/trial/enola/about/over/
A project by students at Lehigh University, this site features primary sources relating to the Smithsonian Institution's exhibit on the plane that dropped the first atomic bomb.

Bibliography

Books

Alperovitz, Gar. *The Decision to Use the Atomic Bomb*. New York: Knopf, 1995.

Andrew, Christopher, and Vasili Mitrokhin. *The Sword and the Shield: The Mitrokhin Archive and the Secret History of the KGB*. New York: Basic Books, 1999.

Barnes-Svarney, Patricia, ed. *The New York Public Library Science Desk Reference*. New York: Macmillan, 1995.

Boyer, Paul. *By the Bomb's Early Light: American Thought and Culture at the Dawn of the Atomic Age*. New York: Pantheon Books, 1985.

Brendon, Piers. *The Dark Valley: A Panorama of the 1930s*. New York: Knopf, 2000.

Dallek, Robert. *Franklin D. Roosevelt and American Foreign Policy, 1932–1945*. New York: Oxford University Press, 1979.

Davis, Kenneth S. *FDR: The New Deal Years, 1933–1937*. New York: Random House, 1986.

Frank, Richard B. *Downfall: The End of the Imperial Japanese Empire*. New York: Penguin Books, 1999.

Harwit, Martin. *An Exhibit Denied: Lobbying the History of the Enola Gay*. New York: Copernicus, 1996.

Herken, Gregg. *The Winning Weapon: The Atomic Bomb in the Cold War 1945–1950*. New York: Knopf, 1980.

Hersey, John. *Hiroshima*. New ed. New York: Alfred A. Knopf, 1985.

Inada, Lawson Fusao, ed. *Only What We Could Carry: The Japanese Internment Experience*. Berkeley, CA: Heyday Books, 2000.

Isaacs, Jeremy, and Taylor Downing. *Cold War: An Illustrated History, 1945–1991*. Boston: Little, Brown and Co., 1998.

Kelly, Cynthia C., ed. *The Manhattan Project*. New York: Black Dog & Leventhal Publishers, 2007.

Lifton, Robert Jay, and Greg Mitchell. *Hiroshima in America: A Half Century of Denial*. New York: Avon Books, 1995.

McCullough, David. *Truman*. New York: Simon & Schuster, 1992.

O'Reilly, Charles T., and William A. Rooney. *The Enola Gay and the Smithsonian Institution*. Jefferson, NC: McFarland & Company, 2005.

Ogura, Toyofumi. *Letters from the End of the World: A Firsthand Account of the Bombing of Hiroshima*. Translated by Kisaburo Murakami and Shigeru Fujii. New York: Kodansha International, 1997.

Paterson, Thomas G, J. Garry Clifford, and Kenneth J. Hagan. *American Foreign Relations: A History Since 1895*, vol. II. Boston: Houghton Mifflin, 2000.

Robinson, Greg. *By Order of the President: FDR and the Internment of Japanese Americans*. Cambridge, MA: Harvard University Press, 2001.

Roosevelt, Franklin D. *Great Speeches*. John Grafton, ed. Mineola, NY: Dover, 1999.

Sherwin, Martin J. *A World Destroyed: Hiroshima and Its Legacies*, 3rd ed. Stanford, CA: Stanford University Press, 2003.

Walker, J. Samuel. *Prompt and Utter Destruction: Truman and the Use of Atomic Bombs Against Japan*. Rev. ed. Chapel Hill: University of North Carolina Press, 2004.

Weale, Adrian, ed. *Eye-Witness Hiroshima*. New York: Carroll & Graf, 1995.

Willmott, H.P., Robin Cross, and Charles Messenger. *World War II*. New York: DK. 2004.

Websites

The American Experience
www.pbs.org/wgbh/amex/bomb/film more/reference/extractsof general/html

The Atomic Heritage Foundation
www.atomicheritage.org/index.php?option=com_frontpage &Itemid=1

Auer, James E., and Richard Halloran. "Looking Back at the Bomb." *Parameters*, Spring 1996. U.S. Army War College Quarterly. www.carlisle.army.mil/USAWC/parameters/96spring/sp-essay.htm

"Before Hiroshima," *Time*, 17 September 1945. Time.com www.time.com/time/magazine/article/0,9171,854438,00.html ?promoid=googlep

"The Chain Reaction." The Special Collections Research Center, the University of Chicago Library
www.lib.uchicago.edu/e/spcl/chain.html#b

Coleman, Joseph. "1945 Tokyo Firebombing Left Legacy of Terror, Pain." CommonDreams.org News Center www.commondreams.org/headlines05/0310-08.htm

"Confinement and Ethnicity: An Overview of World War II Japanese American Relocation Sites." National Parks Service www.nps.gov/history/history/online_books/anthropology74/ce3c.htm

Einstein, Albert. "Letter to Franklin D. Roosevelt, 2 August 1939." Argonne National Laboratory www.anl.gov/Science_and_Technology/History/Anniversary_Frontiers/aetofdr.html

"Einstein Explains the Equivalence of Energy and Matter," *A. Einstein: Image and Impact*. American Institute of Physics Center for the History of Physics www.aip.org/history/einstein/voice1.htm

Gould, Benina Berger. *Living in the Question? The Berlin Nuclear Crisis Critical Oral History, Part II*. University of California Institute of Slavic, East European, and Eurasian Studies repositories. cdlib.org/cgi/viewcontent.cgi?article=1002&context=iseees

The Hiroshima Maidens. Canadian Broadcasting Company Digital Archives. archives.cbc.ca/version_print.asp?page=1&IDLan=1&IDClip=12162&IDDossier=0&IDCat=394&IDCatPa=264

Hixson, David L. "Godzilla." *St. James Encyclopedia of Pop Culture*. findarticles.com/p/articles/mi_g1epc/is_tov/ai_2419100515

Kristof, Nicholas D. "Hiroshima: A Special Report.; The Bomb: An Act That Haunts Japan and America," *New York Times*, 6 August 1995.
query.nytimes.com/gst/fullpage.html?res=990CE0D91430F93 5A3575BC0A963958260

Lindbergh, Charles. "Our Relationship with Europe." Charles A. Lindbergh: An American Aviator
www.charleslindbergh.com/americanfirst/speech3.asp

The Manhattan Project: An Interactive History. Office of Heritage and History Resources, U.S. Department of Energy
www.cfo.doe.gov/me70/manhattan/index.htm

"Merchants of Death," Historical Minute Essays. United States Senate
www.senate.gov/artandhistory/history/minute/merchants_of_death.htm

National Park Service
www.nps.gov/history/history/online_books/anthropology/74/ce3c/htm

Nuclear Files.org. The Nuclear Age Peace Foundation
www.nuclearfiles.org

"Nuclear Special: 'One Hell of a Big Bang.'" *The Guardian*, 6 August, 2002. Guardian.co.uk
www.guardian.co.uk/world/2002/aug/06/nuclear.japan

Potsdam Declaration. Birth of the Constitution of Japan
www.ndl.go.jp/constitution/e/etc/c06.html

Race for the Superbomb. The American Experience
www.pbs.org/wgbh/amex/bomb/filmmore/reference/primary/
extractsofgeneral.html

Rothman, Steve. "The Publication of 'Hiroshima' in the *New Yorker.*" Herseyhiroshima.com
www.herseyhiroshima.com/index.php

"Sputnik." *Cold War.* CNN Interactive
www.cnn.com/SPECIALS/cold.war/episodes/08/

"Statement by the President Announcing the Use of the A-Bomb at Hiroshima." Harry S. Truman Library and Museum
www.trumanlibrary.org/calendar/viewpapers.php?pid=100

Takaki, Ronald. "The Myth of Military Necessity."
bustingbinaries.com/id21.html

Trinity Atomic Web Site
www.cddc.vt.edu/host/atomic/index.html

Truman, Harry. "Address Before a Joint Session of Congress, March 12, 1947." The Avalon Project
www.yale.edu/lawweb/avalon/trudoc.htm

Virtual Museum of the City of San Francisco
www.sfmuseum.org/hist8/editorial1.html

"Young Men and Bombs," *Time*, 23 July 2005.
www.time.com/time/world/article/0,8599,1086088,00.html

Newspapers

Baldwin, Hanson W. "The Atomic Weapon: End of War Against Japan Hastened But Destruction Sows Seed of Hate," *New York Times*, 7 August, 1945, p. 10.

Laurence, William L. "Stimson Reveals Story of Atom Use," *The New York Times*, 28 January 1947, p. 1.

Lawrence, W. H. "Visit to Hiroshima Proves It World's Most-Damaged City," *The New York Times*, 5 September 1945, pp. 1, 4.

Index

Page numbers in **boldface** are illustrations.

Stalin, Joseph, 53, 54, **54**, 58, 61, 63, **64**, 82
Stimson, Henry, 38, 52, 53, 55, 56, 58, 61, 78, 79, 80, 81, 82, 94, 96
Strassmann, Fritz, 31
Szilard, Leo, 32, **33**, 34, 35, 37, 39, 41, 48, 49, 60

Takaki, Ronald, 95–96
Teller, Edward, 35, 86
testing, 61, **62**, 63, 83, **83**, 85, 87, **87**, 89
Tibbets, Paul, 9, 11, 12, 13, 67, 97
Togo, Shigenori, 66
Treaty of Versailles, 18–19
Truman, Harry, 52–53, 54, 55, 59, **59**, 61, 63, **64**, 68, 70, 81, 83, 86, 87, 94, 95, 96

Uchida, Yoshiko, 47
uranium, 31, 32–33, 35, 38, 39, 40, **40**, 49, 51, 52

Van Kirk, Theodore "Dutch," 14

Walker, J. Samuel, 95
World War I, 18–19, 23, 24
World War II, 6–7, 10, 11, 16, 21, 24, 25, 26, 29, 42, 43, 45, 51, 52, 53, 55, 58, 59–60, 61, 63, 64, 65, 66, **67**, 68–69, **68**, 70, 72, 73, 74, 76, 77, 78, 80, 94, 95, 96, 97, 98, 101

Yalta Conference, 54, **54**
Yamaoka, Michiko, 13

About the Author

A history graduate of the University of Connecticut, free-lance author Michael Burgan has written more than 150 fiction and nonfiction books for children, as well as articles for adults. He has written several books on World War II, the cold war, and U.S. foreign policy. Burgan is a recipient of an Educational Press Association of America award.